HOW MONEY WORKS

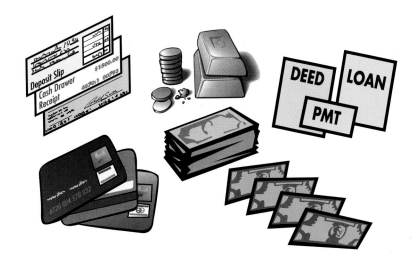

HOW MONEY WORKS

JONATHAN LANSNER

Illustrated by
DAVE FEASEY

Ziff-Davis Press
Emeryville, California

Editor	Valerie Haynes Perry
Technical Reviewer	Michael Hewitt
Project Coordinator	Ami Knox
Page Layout	M.D. Barrera
Illustration	Dave Feasey
Proofreader	Ami Knox
Cover Illustration	Dave Feasey
Cover Design	Regan Honda
Cover Copy	Valerie Haynes Perry
Book Design	Carrie English
Word Processing	Howard Blechman
Indexer	Carol Burbo

Ziff-Davis Press books are produced on a Macintosh computer system with the following applications: FrameMaker®, Microsoft® Word, QuarkXPress®, Adobe Illustrator®, Adobe Photoshop®, Adobe Streamline™, MacLink®*Plus*, Aldus® FreeHand™, Collage Plus™.

If you have comments or questions or would like to receive a free catalog, call or write:
Ziff-Davis Press
5903 Christie Avenue
Emeryville, CA 94608
1-800-688-0448

ISBN 1-56276-291-5

Manufactured in the United States of America
♻ This book is printed on paper that contains 50% total recycled fiber of which 20% is de-inked postconsumer fiber.
10 9 8 7 6 5 4 3 2 1

**To Marianne & Rachel,
the best investments I ever made**

Introduction xi

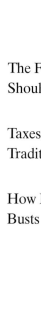

PART 1

The Big Picture
xii

Chapter 1
Money: The Green Stuff 4

Chapter 2
Regulation: Who's Watching
the Store? 8

Chapter 3
Deregulation: The Seed for
So Many Choices 16

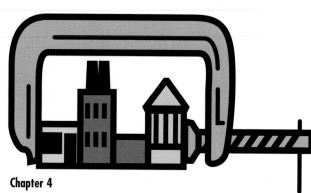

Chapter 4
The Federal Reserve: Why
Should You Care about It? . . 24

Chapter 5
Taxes: An American
Tradition 28

Chapter 6
How Economic Booms and
Busts Happen 32

PART 2

At the Bank
40

Chapter 7
Bank Accounts: A Family's
Financial Backbone 44

Chapter 8
Interest Rates: The Price You
Pay for Money 48

Chapter 9
Checking Accounts: Old and
Reliable 54

Chapter 10
How ATMs Didn't Change
the World 58

Chapter 11
Credit Cards: Plastic That
Changed the World 62

Chapter 12
How the Loan Approval
Process Works 66

Chapter 13
How Credit Reports
Work 70

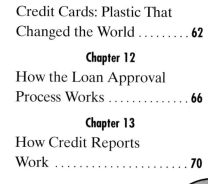

PART 3

Playing the Markets
74

Chapter 14
How the Stock Market
Works.........................78

Chapter 15
Bonds: More Than Just
Interest Rates...............88

Chapter 16
Cash Investments:
For Safety's
Sake........94

Chapter 17
How Commodity Markets
Work........................98

Chapter 18
Mutual Funds: The Small
Investors' Playground......102

Chapter 19
How to Make Sense of Stock
Market Indexes...........112

PART 4

Pocketbook Issues
116

Chapter 20
Home, Sweet Home 120

Chapter 21
Insurance: The Not-So-
Comforting Choices 128

Chapter 22
Retirement:
The Biggest Job...........134

PART 5

Revamping Your Finances
146

Chapter 23
Compound Interest:
The Most Powerful Element
of Finance..................150

Chapter 24
Planning Your Financial
Roadmap 154

Chapter 25
Why $1 Million Isn't What It
Used to Be.................166

Index.......................170

As some finishing touches were being applied to this book in December 1994, the region where I live and work as a journalist, Orange County, California, declared bankruptcy. It is perhaps the largest municipal financial debacle ever. At the heart of the problem was a misguided investment bet that cost the county taxpayers billions—yes, billions—of dollars. The ignorance and indifference of both taxpayers and the public officials up until the troubles became public cries out as a lesson for why you should better educate yourself about the true impact that money can have on your life.

In that spirit, I have to commend the folks at Ziff-Davis Press for expanding their publishing product line into the world of finance. I can't tell you how many times a Ziff-Davis product has helped me figure out how a computer works. I hope you find this book equally helpful. I am eternally grateful to the staff at Ziff-Davis Press who really made this book possible, most notably Valerie Haynes Perry, the development editor who translated my jargon into readable prose; Dave Feasey, the illustrator who translated my stick figures and bar charts into exciting illustrations; and Eric Stone, the acquisitions editor who chose me to take on this project.

I'd also like to thank the numerous people at too many financial service companies, government agencies, and trade groups plus a slew of money experts and analysts. Combined, they provided me with the wealth of facts, figures, and commentary needed to complete this endeavor.

Jonathan Lansner
Trabuco Canyon, California
March 1995

If you feel totally confused by money, you are not alone. Mammoth changes in the financial world have produced a dizzying array of options, opportunities, and potential pitfalls for every American in the past two decades.

At the start of the 1970s, when it came to money, the typical American household had relatively few choices. For example, almost every banker offered the same interest rate on savings accounts. Today, the most popular savings product going, pools of investors' money known as mutual funds, comes in more than 4,000 varieties.

Money management is undergoing an incredibly complex and confusing shakeup in the United States and worldwide. Changes in how the nation's economy is watched by the government creates new rules. Switches in the financial packages employers make with their workers creates new choices. Revolutions in the technology and marketing of money creates an overwhelming variety of new products. And old economic comfort blankets like banks, insurance companies, company pensions and even Social Security seem to be shaky.

What makes it all even more unnerving is that there is no easy way to learn how to keep up with the maddening financial changes. Getting a grasp on how money works—whether it be understanding the economic system or your own family finances—takes time. You'll need to educate yourself to get up to speed on money matters, then you'll have to stay current so you can make better decisions that could alter how you pay for your child's education or how well you live in retirement. You'll have some successes and you will make mistakes. If you are any good at this money game, you will learn from both the good and the bad.

Think of *How Money Works* as your owner's manual for taking care of money. This book serves a purpose similar to that of an owner's manual that comes with a personal computer or a new car. All of these handbooks tell you how to run the machine, offering troubleshooting advice if something goes wrong. *How Money Works* isn't the only help you'll need, but it will put you on the right road.

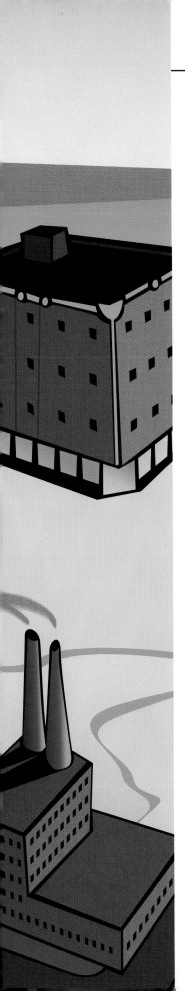

THE BIG PICTURE

CONTENTS

Chapter 1: Money: The Green Stuff
4

Chapter 2: Regulation: Who's Watching the Store?
8

Chapter 3: Deregulation: The Seed for So Many Choices
16

Chapter 4: The Federal Reserve: Why Should You Care
about It?
24

Chapter 5: Taxes: An American Tradition
28

Chapter 6: How Economic Booms and Busts Happen
32

S O, JUST WHERE does money fit into the economic scene? It's certainly more than the green stuff in your wallet, the coins that make the laundry room machinery work, and the plastic cards that buy goods and get cash from a teller machine. Look at money this way: it's the lubricant that keeps the economic motor humming.

At its simplest, the economy can be viewed as a marionette pulled by three strings: Supply, how many goods are available; demand, who wants how much; and price, money's twin cousin, how much is paid for goods and services.

First, let's look at supply's impact on the economy. Think of when something you need or want is in short supply. So, if there's less supply of a good, and demand stays the same, what happens to the price? Remember the oil shortage? Or when the logging industry stopped harvesting trees because of endangered species laws? Or shopping at the supermarket for salad ingredients at Thanksgiving? Bet you paid dearly for gasoline, two-by-fours, and bland tomatoes. Or think of summertime when everybody grows zucchini and the green squash is practically given away by the grocers.

Next, consider demand's role in this game. Let's say supply stays stable and demand surges. Try to get a ticket to that big sporting event or sold-out rock concert. Or buy a home when everyone else is in a panic to do so. You know what happens: the price goes up. Big time. On the flip side, when demand dries up like a prune, what happens to the red-and-green ribbons the day after Christmas? Or who wants to be the owner of the fourth or fifth or sixth house to go on sale on just one block? It's likely that prices will suffer—or goods will be taken off the market until sufficient demand returns again.

But don't assume that price is just a passive response to supply and demand. Remember the last big sale at your local department store? Remember the lines? That's price's impact on demand for goods. Or, think of a time when the price of a favorite item or service was suddenly jerked higher. Did you cut back or eliminate that purchase? That, too, is price's impact on demand. Say the higher price sticks. Don't be surprised if other merchants soon begin to offer the same goods or services because either the higher price brings a fat profit or competitors will try to undercut the high-price merchant. These changes in price can also affect supply.

This book could probably be a pamphlet if supply, demand, and price completely explained money matters. Because this is not the case, let's take a glance at two other major forces in the economic marketplace: competition and government.

Competition is all about winning over customers. When competition is hot, prices often fall. It can be quite obvious, like airlines jockeying for your business. So-called "fare wars" often take place during dead periods as deep discounts are offered for mid-week flights or when few people take vacations. Why? Airplanes still have the same number of seats on slow days as they do on the day before Christmas. But economic rules tell you that airfares may fall when demand is less. Conversely, don't expect a bargain when everyone goes home to visit Mom for the holidays.

Competition can also exist as a subtle means of substituting one good or service for another. For example, what happens when the price of wood rises and you need some shelving? All of a sudden, plastic or metal shelves become a viable alternative. This substitution process often keeps the prices of interchangeable goods and services in line with each other.

Now turn your thoughts to businesses that are *not* driven by competition. Your household utility company is one good example. What do you do if the electric bill is too high? Typically, you can't go to another utility because no one else can link up energy to your home. So, either you conserve energy or sit in the dark and cold. Of course, there used to be just one telephone company, too. Today, people say there are too many phone companies. But long-distance phone rates have tumbled since the government broke up American Telephone & Telegraph.

Now, let us consider the image of the federal government playing in the economic sandbox. This giant force takes on roles from economic police to huge borrower and from economic policy leader to mammoth collector and distributor of wealth.

In its role as top economic cop, the government tries to keep the nation's businesses, industries, and financial system cool, calm, and collected. For example, the Federal Trade Commission tries to ensure that no business becomes so powerful in its industry that it might dictate price and supply, while the Federal Reserve Board tries to moderate surges in interest rates and consumer prices.

The government makes its mark in the marketplace as well. Military needs created an entire industry for defense contractors, which made millions of jobs available. But hopes for worldwide peace in the 1990s are translating into smaller military needs that will cost thousands of defense workers their jobs.

Finally, ponder how taxes affect the economy. When a "luxury tax" was imposed on items like boats and furs in 1991, demand for these expensive goods plummeted. In 1993, Congress had to remove this tax to save the industries that made those items.

Money: The Green Stuff

THE U.S. DOLLAR wasn't always the most desirable currency on the globe, nor was it the first form of U.S. legal tender. Notes that were issued by the Second Continental Congress in 1775 were the government's first attempt at currency. These notes were redeemable into Spanish dollars. The costs of the Revolutionary War with England along with limited taxing abilities quickly made the new government's currency virtually worthless.

U.S. currency continued to have headaches after independence was won. In the mid-19th century paper currency in America was a blizzard of 7,000 different regional issues from local banks. But financial instability at those banks left many people with worthless paper. Things were only marginally better for the U.S. government by 1862, when it was fighting off bankruptcy and a Civil War. This is also when the government issued its first national currency, United States Notes, which had the distinctive look that led to the "greenback" nickname.

As the Civil War erupted, however, general confidence in U.S. paper money was so low that the government was forced to offer greater insurance that its currency would be valid. Because people have long viewed gold as a financial security blanket, in 1865, Gold Certificates were issued. The certificates, redeemable into gold equal to the bill's denomination, were an attempt to calm fears about the government's financial security. They remained part of the American currency until 1933. Silver Certificates were inaugurated in 1878. As recently as 1968, Americans could get silver for Silver Certificates from the U.S. Treasury Department.

After the Civil War, two more financial panics (in 1893 and 1907) led to the formation in 1913 of the Federal Reserve Board. This national central bank manages and distributes the nation's money. The Federal Reserve backed its U.S. currency, Federal Reserve Notes, with purchases of equal amounts of U.S. Treasury bonds. This is still the case today.

Nowadays, people take American paper currency for granted because it is universally accepted and widely available. Most of us instinctively accept the worth of currency without questioning who actually stands behind the pieces of green paper. But the banking system could not have single-handedly produced today's powerful U.S. dollar. Add up great military might plus immense economic muscle, and you have the formula for putting the U.S. dollar on the world's financial pedestal.

The Anatomy of a Dollar Bill

The U.S. dollar is no ordinary piece of paper. It's made of cotton and linen rags and has a pliable feel to it. There are red and blue fibers embedded in the paper to discourage counterfeiting. The bill was 7.42 inches by 3.13 inches until 1929, when the current 6.14 inches by 2.61 inches format was adopted. The intricate design and printing not only qualify the bill as art, but also help to foil counterfeiters. The U.S. Secret Service, better known as the personal protectors of the president and other top U.S. officials, got its start in 1865 as the nation's counterfeiting watchdog—a role it still holds today. Here is a detailed look at some of the nooks and crannies of a dollar bill.

George Washington, the nation's first president, adorns the $1 bill. But whose face is on the other bills still in circulation? Thomas Jefferson ($2), Abraham Lincoln ($5), Alexander Hamilton ($10), Andrew Jackson ($20), Ulysses Grant ($50), and Benjamin Franklin ($100). Want tougher trivia? Name the faces on the out-of-circulation bills: William McKinley ($500), Grover Cleveland ($1,000), James Madison ($5,000), Salmon Chase ($10,000), and Woodrow Wilson ($100,000 bill, briefly used by bankers in the 1930s).

Today, 99 percent of all U.S. paper currency is Federal Reserve Notes, meaning that the U.S. central bank, the Federal Reserve, will make good on the bill. There are a small amount of U.S. Notes in circulation, which are direct obligations of the U.S. Treasury. Gold Certificates and Silver Certificates— bills once payable in those metals—are now collectibles.

Small capital letter and numeral tell the plate position the bill had while being printed.

This emblem and number tell you which of 12 regional Federal Reserve Banks issued the bill. The regional banks and their letter/number codes are Boston (1,A); New York (2, B), Philadelphia (3,C), Cleveland (4,D), Richmond (5,E), Atlanta (6,F), Chicago (7,G), St. Louis (8,H), Minneapolis (9,I), Kansas City (10,J), Dallas (11, K), and San Francisco (12,L).

The series date signifies the year of the bill's original design or its last major remake. Minor revisions are marked by the addition of a small letter under the date. Unlike coins, there is no marking on a bill stating the year in which it was printed, although the signature of the Secretary of the Treasury at the time of issue can help you date it.

Each bill of a particular printing series has a unique serial number. The first letter of the serial number tells you which Federal Reserve Bank issued the bill.

These letters and numbers tell you which printing plate produced this dollar. The large letter always matches the plate position letter in the upper-left corner of the bill. The letters *FW* mean that the bill was printed in Fort Worth, Texas, the Bureau of Engraving and Printing. Fort Worth opened in 1991 as the second printing plant of the nation's currency maker, Washington, D.C., being the first.

The U.S. Treasury seal is green on a Federal Reserve Note but red on a U.S. Note.

The phrase "In God We Trust" had been on U.S. coins since 1864. It took an act of Congress in 1957 to get the phrase printed on paper currency.

Both sides of the Great Seal of the United States, the only two-sided government seal in the world, are on the back of the $1 bill. Other bills in circulation have the following imprints on their backs:$2 (signing of the Declaration of Independence), $5 (Lincoln Memorial), $10 (U.S. Treasury), $20 (White House), $50 (U.S. Capitol), and $100 (Independence Hall).

CHAPTER 2

Regulation: Who's Watching the Store?

THERE'S ONE GIVEN in the financial world: There will always be plenty of rules for the businesses that handle money. "Regulation" is the fancy word for these rules; it is the government's oversight of businesses and their practices.

Few industries are regulated more strictly than the financial-service industry. In fact, some bankers may have as many as five agencies serving as their primary regulators, not to mention a dozen or so others who may oversee everything from workplace rules to acquiring permits for a new branch.

The two main reasons for the heavy regulation of the world of money are keeping financial institutions in good economic health and making sure the investing and saving public is protected from unscrupulous operators. These measures are in place to ensure a healthy financial system and a high standard of living in the United States.

Unfortunately, much of the framework for the nation's financial regulation is the result of rules and laws that were written after a series of economic crises. In the mid-19th century, a wave of bank failures started the movement to regulate the nation's banking industry. Banking and investment problems of the Great Depression of the 1930s were the catalysts for regulation of the investment business and for the establishment of federal deposit insurance. In the early 1990s, a series of failures of large life insurance companies created political pressure to start federal oversight of that industry. But legislation that was proposed to create federal regulation of life insurance failed to get enough votes in Congress to become law. As a result, life insurance is the only major money business that escapes federal oversight. The industry is solely regulated by state authorities.

The tendency of Congress to handle financial-industry regulation on a crisis-by-crisis basis created a patchwork quilt of various policies. For example, five federal agencies oversee the nation's banks, savings and loans, and credit unions, which provide similar services. Another layer of regulation exists for all these bankers at the state level. Two more U.S. bureaucracies watch over the nation's stock, bond, and commodities markets, while two industry groups serve as a self-policing mechanism for the financial markets as well.

There is more. If someone peddling investments or goods lies about the product, the Federal Trade Commission (FTC) might step in and punish the violator. And if any retailer, banker, broker, or other investment salesperson breaks anti-fraud laws, the U.S. Justice Department or state attorney general offices can bring criminal charges. However, financial regulation usually guarantees only that a money-related product appears to be fair. It does not ensure that the government is standing by to help out financially if something goes wrong.

Protection like federal deposit insurance gives to savers is a rarity. This coverage pays up to $100,000 if a federally insured banking institution goes broke. The only other comparable federal protection is the backing workers get from the Pension Benefit Guaranty Corp. This organization will pay retirees part of their private pension payments if the worker's old company that promised the benefits goes out of business.

Consumers get a good deal of regulatory support when it comes to the lending practices of different financial institutions. Various federal and state laws try to make sure that you get equitable treatment when borrowing money. For example, it is illegal for a lender to discriminate against a borrower because of their race, gender, or age. Other regulations require that the terms of a loan, its length, and the interest rate charged as well as any associated fees, must all be clearly spelled out. There are also laws that give you rights to find out what went wrong if you have a dispute with a lender or if you are turned down for credit. Some states even continue to enforce "usury" laws that limit how much interest a lender can charge.

Investments, too, are often subject to considerable government oversight. Companies selling stocks or bonds must get their offerings approved by the U.S. Securities and Exchange Commission (SEC), the nation's chief investments regulator. The same goes for the sale of shares in mutual funds, which are the popular pools of investors' money that trade stocks and bonds. However, SEC approval of a stock, bond, or fund does not guarantee that the investor will ever get a dime back from the investment. Instead, it only means the SEC believes that the issuing company has given the investor a fair picture of the risks involved in their stocks, bonds, or funds.

Those who sell investments to the public are also subject to regulatory oversight. For instance, investment brokerages that peddle stocks and bonds are licensed and their finances are monitored to ensure that they can stay in business. Many of the professionals at these firms deal individually with investors. These professionals must pass tests to get a securities license that permits them to sell regulated financial products.

Furthermore, the fund industry has many regulations such as one that requires a third-party trustee to handle a mutual funds' cash and investments in order to increase the investor's protection. The government even watches the stock, bond, and commodity exchanges, too, in an attempt to keep investment trading honest and reliable.

The average saver or investor should do some homework to understand the apparent alphabet soup of agencies that actually can be valuable resources. Some of these regulators offer low-cost information on basic money matters. Other groups serve as a clearinghouse for information about the integrity of an institution you may be dealing with. You can also turn to regulators if an investment or financial service goes awry.

The following list of U.S. agencies and industry watchdog groups that oversee financial matters and addresses may be of some use to you:

Regulator	Address
Commodity Futures Trading Commission	2033 K St., NW, Washington, DC 20581
Federal Deposit Insurance Corporation	550 17th St., NW, Washington, DC 20551
Federal Trade Commission	6th St. and Pennsylvania Ave., Washington, DC 20580
Federal Reserve System	20th and C Streets, NW, Washington, DC 20219
Housing and Urban Development Department	451 7th St., NW, Washington, DC 20401
Internal Revenue Service	1111 Constitution Ave., NW, Washington DC 20224
National Association of Insurance Commissioners	444 N. Capitol St., NW, Suite 309, Washington, DC 20001
North American Securities Administrators Association	1 Massachusetts Ave., Suite 310, Washington, DC 20001
National Association of Securities Dealers	1735 K St., Washington, DC 20006
National Credit Union Administration	1775 Duke St., Alexandria, VA 22314
National Futures Association	200 W. Madison St., Suite 1600, Chicago IL 60606
New York Stock Exchange	11 Wall St., New York, NY 10005
Office of the Comptroller of the Currency	250 E St., SW, Washington, DC 20219
Office of Thrift Supervision	1700 G St., NW, Washington, DC 20551
Securities and Exchange Commission	450 Fifth St., NW, Washington, DC 20549

The Players: Financial Institutions at a Glance

Here's a look at who's who in the financial service game. If you think it's getting harder to tell them apart these days, you're right.

Funds

Open-end funds are the most popular type. They pool investors' money to make investments according to a prescribed strategy such as stocks, fixed-income (concentrating on bonds), or money markets (stocks with ultrasafe securities). They continually sell new shares.

Closed-end funds also pool investors' money to make investments based on a prescribed strategy. However, they typically raise money in a one-time share sale.

Insurers

Life insurance protects against loss of income from death and disability. It also offers investment products such as universal life and annuities, both designed to build retirement nest eggs.

Property-casualty insurance protects homes, businesses, and cars against losses from theft, fires, weather damage, and accidents. It also protects owners from liability suit losses, such as one for injuries from tripping on one's sidewalk.

Medical insurance consists of two broad types. One lets patients choose their own doctor and typically pays the insured 80 percent of medical costs. The other, health maintenance organizations (HMOs) and preferred provider organizations (PPOs), limits physician choice to the insurer's own list, but only charges patients a modest visit fee, which is often around $10.

Brokers

Full-service stock brokerages provide customers with financial advice from a personal representative who can cull information from the brokerage's own research staff. Once a customer decides on an investment, the brokerage then executes the requested trade. These firms also raise money for corporations and governments through the sale of new stocks and bonds.

Discount stock brokerages provide customers with little advice or research capability. In return, the commission on trades executed by the discount brokerage is greatly reduced.

SCOREBOARD

	Insured deposits	Checking accounts	Home loans	Auto loans	Stock trades	Mutual funds	Life insurance
Commercial banks							
Savings & loans							
Credit unions							
Stock brokerages							
Mutual funds							
Life insurers							

Key: Widely available   Sometimes available   Rarely available

The Scoreboard

This chart highlights some of the overlaps between key institutions and various services. A green dot means that a service is widely available at that institution; a yellow dot means that it is sometimes available; and a red dot means that it is rarely available.

Exchanges

Stock exchanges are places where people meet to trade stocks. Trades are conducted by a third party (specialist) who matches buy and sell orders or by buyers and sellers getting together.
Over-the-counter exchanges are informal or electronic networks that are used to trade stocks and bonds. Traders can pick the best prices from posted buy and sell orders via telephone or computer hook-up. Nasdaq (National Association of Securities Dealers Automated Quotations) is the best known network for stock trades.
Commodity exchanges allow businesspeople to hedge against price swings in everything from pork to gold to interest rates. Meanwhile, speculators try to profit from those price swings. Traders meet in "pits" where they call out their buy and sell orders.

Housing

Real estate agents help in shopping or negotiating for a home or other real estate.
Mortgage bankers rely on private sources of money rather than bank or S&L deposits.
Title insurers protect buyers and sellers from unknown financial or ownership claims against property.

Bankers

Traditional commercial banks once concentrated on business banking and personal checking accounts. Today, they offer consumers a full array of products and services, from home loans to mutual funds.
Savings and loans (S&Ls) are the traditional mortgage lenders and favorite savings place for Americans. The ranks were thinned greatly by 1980s S&L financial crisis, making the remaining industry almost indistinguishable from banks.
Savings banks are a cross between an S&L and a commercial bank, typically with an orientation towards consumer products and services. Many S&Ls became savings banks to flee the industry's stigma after the crisis.
Credit unions' membership is frequently limited to people who share the same workplace, industry, or neighborhoods. Credit unions are best known for auto loans. Typically, they offer a limited product line.

The Regulatory Landscape: An Alphabet Soup of Oversight

The nation's world of money is carefully watched by various federal and state agencies as well as industry-supported watchdog groups. The regulators can be quite helpful (often with free literature) in letting savers or consumers gain a better understanding of what they may be buying or investing in. Don't be shy! Feel free to contact these or other regulatory bodies to learn more about the economy and the money system. Consult the listing on page 11.

Commercial banks are federally regulated by the OCC (Office of the Comptroller of the Currency), the "Fed" (Federal Reserve Board), and the FDIC (Federal Deposit Insurance Corp.), which oversees the deposit insurance fund. Various state agencies regulate, too.

Savings and loans are federally regulated by the OTS (Office of Thrift Supervision). Various state agencies regulate, too. The FDIC (Federal Deposit Insurance Corp.) oversees the deposit insurance fund.

Credit unions are federally regulated by the NCUA (National Credit Union Administration). Deposit fund oversight is handled by the NCUSIF (National Credit Union Share Insurance Fund). There are some credit unions whose only regulator is their local state banking agency.

Mutual funds are federally regulated by the SEC (Security and Exchange Commission) and an industry-supported watchdog, the NASD (National Association of Securities Dealers). With the soaring popularity of funds, many state agencies have begun to supervise the practices associated with these sales.

Commodity trading is federally regulated by the CFTC (Commodity Futures and Trading Commission). The NFA (National Futures Association), an industry trade group, will resolve investors' disputes with commodity brokers.

Stock exchanges are federally regulated by the SEC (Securities and Exchange Commission).

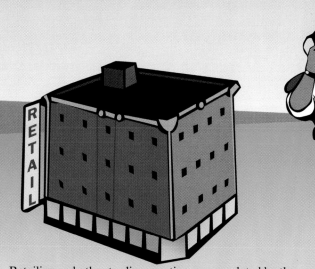

Retailing and other trading practices are regulated by the FTC (Federal Trade Commission). The FTC oversees the fairness of sales presentations and merchant's claims both at the store and through telemarketing about the products and services. State attorney general (AG) offices also make sure retailers aren't cheating consumers.

Stock brokerages are federally regulated by the SEC (Securities and Exchange Commission); the exchanges where the brokerages trade, such as the NYSE (New York Stock Exchange); an industry-supported watchdog, the NASD (National Association of Securities Dealers); and state regulators headed by the NASAA (North American Securities Administrators Association).

Insurance is not subject to federal regulation. State regulation is coordinated by the NAIC (National Association of Insurance Commissioners).

General oversight is conducted by other federal agencies with supervisory powers that touch the economy, too. They include the U.S. Treasury Department (oversees many banking and investment issues); the Justice Department (acts as the legal expert for other U.S. agencies and prosecutes financial crimes) and the Labor Department (oversees workplace issues). Many state agencies, corporations departments, or secretaries of state watch local business issues.

The economy is regulated by the Fed (Federal Reserve Board). The FTC (Federal Trade Commission) watches the economy to make sure no company is overbearing any one industry, either nationwide or in one region, with unfair or monopolistic business practices. Finally, there's the tax collector, the IRS (Internal Revenue Service); and the U.S. Departments of Commerce, Agriculture, and Interior, three agencies that regulate everything from foreign trade to farms to logging rules.

Real-estate issues for Uncle Sam are regulated by HUD, the federal Department of Housing and Urban Development. But the bulk of the oversight comes from various state agencies that license and watch property sales and investments.

CHAPTER
3

Deregulation: The Seed for So Many Choices

F YOU FEEL totally confused by too many financial alternatives, blame it all on deregulation—the government's surrender of its broad supervisory and rule-making powers over the economic and business world.

The government once controlled many aspects of the financial world: from how much interest your banker could offer on savings accounts to the terms of your home mortgage. Today, the power of the marketplace controls the terms of most financial deals.

The transition has not been easy. During the past three decades of deregulation, there was no grand plan to the federal government's surrender of its reins over the world of money. Deregulation was much more a reaction to changing technologies and world economics than the product of any master plan.

The sharply rising consumer prices in the early 1970s and the subsequent soaring interest rates of the late 1970s helped expose the weakness of government's management of the business world. Regulators were often unable to keep up with fast-moving economies. Add to that the ability of financial institutions to enhance the bookkeeping involved with complex products, thanks to rapidly improving computer technology. Plus, savvy marketing techniques were arriving at money industries, such as banks, insurance agencies, and mutual funds. All of these events resulted in a formula for a dramatic transformation of economics and business practices.

A glance back to 1969 would reveal political turbulence laying subtle groundwork for this financial revolution: Nixon was in the White House, and the war in Vietnam was still going on. Yet, managing family money matters was relatively simple then. If you stashed a few dollars away in 1969, you got a token gift from your bank as a "Thank You" for opening a new account. However, few savers went bank-to-bank to shop interest rates in 1969 because there was little competition for interest rates after 1966. This was when the government took away bankers' freedom to set rates for deposits. Regulators feared that bankers would pay too much interest on deposits and not take in enough interest on loans, a trend that could make institutions unprofitable.

If you were shopping for a home loan in 1969, the choices were limited, too. Virtually every lender offered only one type of mortgage: a fixed-rate loan, typically a 30-year arrangement. Adjustable-rate loans, a mainstay of today's home finance market, were dramatically curtailed by government rules in 1969. Back then, regulators didn't think that homeowners' finances could handle fluctuating home payments. Today, roughly one in three mortgages has variable terms that set monthly payments to change in step with a predetermined benchmark interest rate.

The prices of two key economic and investment variables were also fixed by the government in 1969: gold and foreign currencies. Economic experts see Nixon's unchaining of gold and currency prices in 1971 as the birth of the deregulatory movement. Today, gold and foreign currencies are watched by both professional traders and small investors alike. Gold bullion and shares in gold-mining companies are popular as insurance hedges against the damage inflation can do to an investor's wealth.

However, the move toward deregulation didn't happen overnight. There was no landmark legislation or presidential order. Rather, an erratic pattern of new products and regulatory rules built a financial patchwork during the next two decades. Consider the money market mutual fund as an example. Started in 1972, these professionally managed pools of investors' money offered some of the safety of a bank account—and interest rates not tethered by government regulation. When interest rates soared in the late 1970s to peak above 20 percent in 1980–1981, money funds' yields could jump accordingly. Money funds took in billions of dollars from accounts at banks and savings and loans (S&Ls). Bank accounts' yields, however, stayed artificially low because of the 1966 limit on competition. The result was an unprecedented flow of savers' money out of banks and S&Ls to the money funds. This forced government regulators to let bankers in the late 1970s begin competing for depositors' money by allowing them to offer whatever interest rates savers would demand.

The economic trends of the late 1970s were unkind to the nation's S&Ls, whose traditional services were taking in deposits and making home loans. Remember, until 1981, the S&Ls only made fixed-rate mortgages. So, when an S&L's expenses (interest paid on deposits) exceeded its income (interest collected on loans), huge losses were inevitable.

In the early 1980s, lawmakers tried to rescue the ailing S&L industry by letting S&L managers expand beyond servicing deposits and mortgages. What resulted, says Iowa congressman Jim Leach, was "the greatest public policy mistake in history." While legislation protected savers by means of federal deposit insurance, many S&Ls quickly went under because their managers could not handle the new business opportunities. These prospects ran the gamut from unsupervised deposit interest rates to investing in everything from hamburger chains to luxury hotels to building entire cities. The S&Ls' losses were so huge that in 1989 the U.S. government was forced to reregulate the industry, although the terms on savings accounts and loans were left untouched.

New rules greatly limited S&Ls' business activities, primarily to their traditional deposit-taking and home mortgage-lending operations. Scores of S&L swindlers were jailed. The bill for damages, which totaled half a trillion dollars after interest costs, went to the American taxpayers.

But, although the S&L damage was unrivaled in magnitude, it was not the only turmoil created by deregulation. Think of stockbrokers. A traditional brokerage offers a great deal of service, from personalized investment selection to researching the quality of various investment alternatives. Investors paid for these services by paying a commission to their stockbroker each time they made a purchase or a sale.

The 1970s were not good economic years for the U.S., and a bad economy made for falling stock prices, which pushed stock investors to other types of investments. To generate new business, in 1975 the brokerage industry obtained government approval to unchain previously regulated commissions charged for buying and selling stocks. The new rules that resulted were the backbone of an entirely new style of investment firm, the so-called "discount stock brokerage."

The new discount brokerages were no-frills operations. No fancy offices, no glossy brochures—customers didn't even have their own broker. In return for reduced service, the discount brokerage offered extremely low commissions. Furthermore, a client received no advice from the discount brokerage; this business was styled for the do-it-yourself investor. This innovation led to the following personal choice: Do you go to a broker for advice, or do you do the research on your own?

All told, the credit card business may be the most unusual case of how a corner of the financial world was shaken by the phenomenon of deregulation.

Today, for many Americans, not a month goes by without an offer of a new Visa or MasterCard, the full-service credit cards that are so popular because they eliminate the need for a wallet's worth of individual stores' credit cards. Visa and MasterCard do not set the terms for the cards that carry their logos. That chore is left up to the company that issues the consumer a card. Visa and MasterCard only serve as information go-betweens, working like cooperatives to make sure the billings and receipts from card transactions get to the right places.

Credit card companies are governed by the state where the card operations are headquartered, not where the cardholder resides. In the 1980s several states—notably South Dakota and Delaware—began actively luring credit card companies in other states to relocate their operations. States such as South Dakota and Delaware enticed card companies by eliminating legal limits on how much interest could be charged to cardholders. As a result, many bankers moved just their credit card operations to card-friendly states. This is why one month, your bill came from your hometown and the next, it might come from a state like South Dakota. This state became the home of Citibank's credit card operation, the world's largest.

For consumers, these events were bad news. Credit card interest rates stayed high, near 20 percent, even after those high interest rates of the early 1980s had worked themselves out of the economy.

Enter AT&T, the old telephone company. In 1991, AT&T won the right from the government to offer a MasterCard through a tiny bank in Georgia. This ruling marked the first time that a large nonfinancial company was able to beat government prohibitions barring them from what had previously been only bankers' business. AT&T itself experienced with deregulation from the 1984 breakup of its old nationwide telephone network, became one of the ten largest credit card issuers almost overnight. Its secret: A card that had no annual service fee.

This time, deregulation made the consumer a winner. The success of AT&T lured other players into the credit card business either as issuers or cosponsors, like General Motors' GM Card that offers rebates on car purchases to frequent card users. Meanwhile, traditional card companies are being forced to repackage their products with lower interest rates and smaller annual fees to stay competitive.

So, the next time your mail carrier brings you a credit card offering, think of it as an economics lesson in deregulation—one your banker might want you to soon forget.

Of course, this deregulation thing has created a bit of a crazy world. A world where that once-regulated $35-an-ounce gold in 1971 could be worth $850 an ounce in 1980 after deregulation. It's a world where a free-floating U.S. dollar could fluctuate so much that although it bought 359 yen in 1971 and 250 yen in the early 1980s, it was worth just 100 yen in 1994. It's a world where some Americans who want a variable-rate mortgage can get a loan that ties their monthly payments to changes in a London-based interest rate known as LIBOR (London Interbank Offered Rate).

But don't complain about too many choices or too many variables. That's the price one has to pay for a competitive marketplace.

How Deregulation Changed the Money Landscape

It's been a rocky road through the financial world's era of change. Here's a look at key dates in the somewhat erratic and unplanned evolution during the past 30 years and the underlying economic conditions that caused some of those changes.

Early 70s: U.S. enacted price-and-wage controls as inflation passed 6%. Interest rates began a long climb, heightening consumer awareness of low, regulated bank interest rates.

1971: President Nixon freed the prices of gold and foreign currencies from the U.S. government's control, granting average Americans the right to invest in gold.

1972: This was the birth of the money market mutual fund. These funds allowed small savers to receive interest rates once reserved for the wealthy.

1966: An ironic start to our trip because this year saw one of the last government attempts to regulate interest rates on savings accounts. A growing, wartime economy had increased interest rates to what, at that time, were rarely seen heights, over 6 percent. This caused bank regulators to take away bankers' ability to offer high deposit rates. The regulators feared that stiff competition for deposits might allow bankers to imperil the safety of their own institutions. This move would eventually cripple the S&L industry's ability to raise money for its mortage-lending business.

Mid 70s: Rising consumer prices and interest rates hurt the economy. That created six money-losing years for stocks and the stock-brokerage industry.

1975: Profits at companies that sold or traded stocks plummeted. A weak U.S. economy hurt stock prices. To stimulate new stock-trading business, the government allowed stock brokerages for the first time to compete for clients by varying the commissions and fees charged for advice and trading services. This provided the seed for the so-called "discount stock brokerage."

Mid-60s: This was the first bout with financial uncertainty in the U.S. in years. Inflation hit a 15-year high at 4% and interest rates reached 40-year highs at 6%.

1978: The Internal Revenue Service allowed new retirement savings plans, dubbed "401(k)" from the section of Tax Code that created the new programs. Previously, companies hired investment professionals to manage their workers' pension. Now, 401(k) programs force workers to manage their own retirement nest eggs. Employees can contribute money from their paychecks into 401(k) plans, with employers adding only modest amounts. The true impact of this opportunity has yet to be fully recognized by most people.

1986: A tax reform act prevented Americans from further using personal interest expenses—such as car or credit card debts—as tax breaks. The only interest expense that was spared was home-related borrowing. This helped to popularize home equity loans, where homeowners take out a second mortgage against any appreciation in their home's value. These new laws also limited tax breaks resulting from personal contributions to Individual Retirement Accounts (IRAs), just five years after IRA deductions were greatly liberated. This cutback helped 401(k) plans to gain favor as a workplace fringe benefit.

1986

Early 80s: Record interest-rate spiked to above 20%. Inflation moderated. Economy went into a deep recession.

Mid-80s: Better times returned. Interest rates fell back to single digits as the U.S. economy, stocks, and real estate boomed.

Late 80s: Bad time for investors as stocks, real estate, and junk bonds crashed. S&Ls were badly hurt by these falls.

1982

1989

1989: Massive S&L losses forced Congress to reregulate the industry. Publicity was so bad that many institutions chose to drop the "savings and loan" moniker from their signage and replaced it with the name "bank."

1982: Congress and regulators expanded S&L business options. S&Ls were freed to build stores and motels and to make bets on stocks and bonds. Meanwhile, bankers were once again freed to set bank accounts' interest rates as they saw fit. Heavy competition for savers' dollars followed.

1991

1981: The fixed-rate S&Ls got the right to offer adjustable-rate mortgages.

1991: AT&T won the right to offer a full-service MasterCard. The AT&T card started a trend that brought credit card competition for customers to new heights. Interest rates and annual fees for credit cards tumbled while cardholder services expanded rapidly.

1981

Early 90s: Weak economy meant few new jobs. And bank interest rates hit 20-year lows at 3% or less—this was a big plus for mutual funds.

1993: Perhaps the biggest beneficiary of all this financial confusion was the mutual fund industry. In 1993, it passed the $2 trillion mark in assets under control, a sum equal to the money held by the nation's banks and S&Ls combined. To show how much mutual funds have grown, note that these investment pools had less than $50 billion in assets in 1970 industrywide.

1993

The Federal Reserve: Why Should You Care about It?

THE FEDERAL RESERVE System (the Fed) serves as the nation's central bank. It functions as an economic and banking overseer as well as a processor of currency and checks. The Fed was formed in 1913 to lend economic strength to the country's financial system. It was created in response to a series of U.S. financial calamities that took place throughout the 19th century.

The Fed's power comes from its freedom to set what economists call "monetary policy," the availability and price of money and credit. It may sound dull, but the Fed's unusual independence from political agendas gives it financial clout that can dramatically affect your standard of living and investments.

Unlike other government agencies or political bodies, the Fed has few political allegiances. Its Board of Governors is composed of political appointees, but the decisions the board makes require no legislative or presidential approval. Certainly, the Fed isn't the only government body with power over the economy. Congress and the president can alter what economists call "fiscal policies"—things like taxes, deficit borrowing, regulatory issues over banking and commerce, and directions in federal spending. But where Congress debates economic issues in public, the Fed does much of its work in secret. The Fed's financial clout makes its chairperson one of the most powerful officials in the world.

Go back to the late 1970s. The U.S. economy was ailing after a decade of sharply rising prices and weak economic growth that produced few new jobs. Fed Chairman Paul Volcker made a bold move: He drastically restricted the availability of money and credit and pushed interest rates to record heights above 20 percent—rates not seen since the Civil War. The reaction was swift. As politicians and citizens called for Volcker's ouster, the economy stalled and fell into recession as factories and service companies laid off workers. A lowered demand for goods resulted from high costs of borrowing and more joblessness. These factors eased inflation, and once inflationary pressures were restrained, the Fed began to slowly restore the availability of money and credit. By 1987, when Volcker voluntarily stepped down as Fed chairman, he was hailed as helping create the 1980s' economic boom, the longest economic upswing since World War II.

This type of maneuvering isn't always productive. Somewhat similar moves at the end of the 1920s were blamed, in part, for starting the Great Depression of the 1930s. So when you realize that the Fed can affect everything from the interest rates on your savings account or mortgage to the chances that you keep your job, you may pay more attention to this seemingly boring agency.

How the Fed Manages the Economy

The Fed's main goal is keeping the economy in balance; it serves as the czar of the role that money plays in this capacity. Moderate growth is the means of maintaining a healthy economy. This situation occurs when the economy creates growing sales of everything from oil tankers to toys and at the same time keeps the economy's inflation rate in check. To make sense of the economic puzzle, the Fed relies on data from other government agencies as well as information gathered from its regional Federal Reserve Banks, which split the nation into 12 areas. Local branch offices help the regional banks provide many of their banking services such as currency distribution and check clearing. Below is a look at the Fed's regional set-up.

Alaska

Seattle

Portland

Helena

Minneapolis ☆9

Buffalo

Boston ☆1

New York ☆2

Detroit Cleveland

Salt Lake City

Chicago ☆7

Pittsburgh

Cincinnati

☆4

Philadelphia ☆3

Baltimore

WASHINGTON

San Francisco ☆12

Denver

Kansas City ☆10

St. Louis ☆8

Louisville

Richmond ☆5

Omaha

Oklahoma City

Memphis Nashville

Charlotte

Los Angeles

Little Rock

Atlanta ☆6

Hawaii

El Paso

Dallas ☆11

Birmingham

Jacksonville

San Antonio Houston

New Orleans

Miami

Puerto Rico

Virgin Islands

The Fed has three other key chores: One, it oversees the distribution of coins and currencies through its regional offices. Two, it is the leading processor of checks, getting them back to the institution used by the check writer. Three, it has regulatory authority over certain commercial banks.

☆ **Regional Headquarters**   ○ **Branch Office**

The Fed's tool in steering the economy is called "monetary policy," the management of interest rates and the supply of money. This policy is directed by the Fed's Federal Open Market Committee (FOMC) that meets throughout the year to put the economy under a microscope. The FOMC is composed of the Federal Reserve's seven-member Board of Governors in Washington, D.C., and five presidents of the regional Federal Reserve Banks. The president of the New York Federal Reserve Bank is always on the FOMC, and the four remaining regional positions rotate among the other 11 Federal Reserve Bank presidents.

After studying mountains of data and having a healthy debate, the FOMC makes its best guess about how the economy is doing and what might correct any problems. Let's assume for this example that there are three possible diagnoses: the U.S. economy is either "Too Hot," "Too Cold," or "Just Right."

"Just Right"
The most common call. In this case, the Fed decides to let the economy take its course until its next scheduled meeting, or until an emergency arises. The FOMC meets eight times a year in Washington, D.C.

"Too Hot"
The Fed finds that the economy is running too fast. Factories and service companies can't hire enough workers. Sales of many goods are booming and raw materials are scarce. Prices of goods and services for both business and consumers are beginning to rise at an alarming rate, a phenomenon called "inflation." The demand for money is strong, so interest rates head higher.

"Too Cold"
The Fed finds that the economy is slumping. Factories and service firms are laying off workers. Raw materials as well as finished products pile up unsold in warehouses. Businesses and consumers are skittish about making big-dollar purchases because of the bleak outlook. The demand for money is minimal so interest rates head lower.

The Fed can alter the nation's money supply by using any of these methods: varying the interest rate (the "discount rate") charged to banks for the large loans they get from the Fed; changing rules that alter how much bankers can lend; and physically modifying the supply of money by buying or selling securities in bond markets. Or the Fed can use a combination of all three strategies.

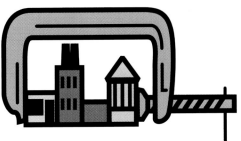

To cool an overheated economy, the Fed will try a "tight monetary policy" to make money less available and raise interest rates. In theory, higher borrowing costs will stunt the demand of both businesses and consumers for goods and services that are in short supply. This would relieve inflation caused by shortages of both raw and finished goods. The risk here is putting the brakes on the economy too harshly and throwing a booming economy into a tailspin.

To pump up a weak economy, the Fed will try a "loose" or "accommodative" monetary policy to make money more available at lower interest rates. Lower borrowing costs may spur companies to build new plants or rehire workers. Consumers may use lower rates to make additional purchases. But lower interest rates don't always work because unemployed workers or shuttered factories have little use for cheap money.

Taxes:
An American Tradition

FOR CITIZENS OF a country that was born from a tax revolt, Americans sure pay a grand sum of taxes. According to the Tax Foundation in Washington, D.C., as of 1994, all federal, state, and local levies have surpassed $2 trillion a year.

After declaring independence from England in 1776, the antitax sentiment in America was so high that the U.S. government taxed infrequently just to pay off debts, such as the costs of wars. It was not until the Civil War broke out that major taxing—including the first income tax—was established. Ever since, government taxes as well as government services overall have exploded.

Today taxes are more than the government bureaucracy's tollbooth on the economic highway. They are a key component of the government's economic policies. Changes in tax laws can be a powerful force in people's money-using habits. For example, ponder the federal income tax cuts put in place in the early 1980s by President Reagan. These cuts fattened the average American's take-home pay and helped create a consumer spending spree that made for the longest period of economic growth since World War II. This example shows how tax cuts can stimulate the economy. Conversely, higher income taxes can put the brakes on the economy, as evidenced by the Bush administration. The result of raising the government's slice of paychecks is diminished buying power.

Several tax-related factors can motivate financial behavior and achieve positive outcomes. So-called "sin" taxes on goods like tobacco or liquor are designed to dissuade people from using these goods. Tax incentives encourage consumers to buy real estate, and the money paid in monthly interest payments lowers income tax bills. Contributions to a 401(k) retirement program or similar savings plans at the workplace are other tax incentives that allow you to stash away money for a retirement nest egg before taxes.

Tax avoidance is an area in which Americans sometimes go overboard. Municipal bonds are an example of this. These bonds are interest-paying obligations of state and local governments that are popular because the income they generate is usually free from state income taxes. However, Internal Revenue Service figures show that one in seven taxpayers who declared tax-free income from municipal bonds did not make enough money to enjoy the benefits of tax-free investments.

The Tax Foundation estimates that the $2 trillion Americans pay in taxes is equal to about 33 percent of the country's earnings. If this figure seems unreasonable, consider France's plight. In France, 49 percent of all taxpayer earnings go to taxes.

How Taxes Work

Do you feel like you pay a lot of taxes? Well, the Tax Foundation of Washington, D.C., says that tax collections in 1994 equaled $7,927 for every man, woman, and child in the U.S. Below is a glance at who collected that money, and how much, based on per-capita figures.

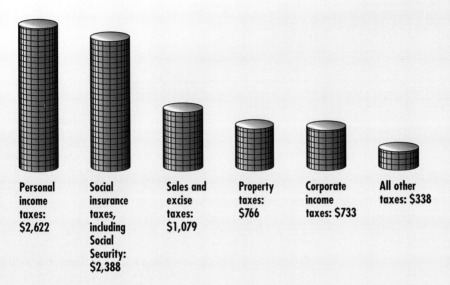

Personal income taxes: $2,622

Social insurance taxes, including Social Security: $2,388

Sales and excise taxes: $1,079

Property taxes: $766

Corporate income taxes: $733

All other taxes: $338

In a climate where raising high-profile taxes can be political suicide, governments at various levels have switched to imposing more subtle taxes. The Tax Foundation found that state and local taxes in 1960 took a bite of the average family's paycheck equal to that of federal taxes. Today, the typical taxpayer pays 50 percent more to local governments than to Uncle Sam. Here's a look at how some of those new local government charges might hit a household.

Budgets for public schools are tight these days. In some parts of the country, public schools with the power to raise taxes are now charging parents for bus service.

To maintain, repair, or build roads, bridges, and tunnels, drivers will find that tolls are rising. In Southern California, bastion of the freeway, system toll roads are a key way to fund new thoroughfares.

Taxes will even get into your safe. Some states have imposed property taxes on the value of investments, such as stocks, bonds, and mutual fund shares.

States are now taxing drivers on more than the right to drive—they've established taxes based on the value of a car, making new and/or expensive vehicles even pricier to maintain.

Many municipalities have begun to tax consumers through their water, telephone, or power bills.

While property taxes are quite old, many municipalities are digging deeper into real estate by taxing new construction as well as remodeling jobs with huge fees for plan approvals, construction inspections, and utility hook-ups.

Another new source of tax revenue is broadening the definition of sales taxes. Everything from out-of-state mail-order goods to junk food (groceries are typically unscathed) has been targeted.

Taking out the garbage has become a premium service. Even traditional local government services like sanitation, police, and fire can cost a homeowner on a per-visit basis in various municipalities.

Local governments have become doggedly tough on collecting small fees, whether it be for pet licenses or other so-called "user" fees, where only residents who use or require a service pay a fee.

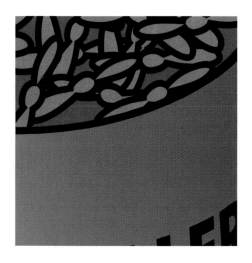

How Economic Booms and Busts Happen

FORCES FROM BOTH inside and outside the nation's economy—plus a bit of human psychology—often push the country into economic "boom" (fast growth) periods and "bust" periods ("recessions" and "depressions"). These "business cycles" consist of periods of economic growth that eventually peak. A period of decline follows, until that trend finally hits a bottom. Then, another growth period begins.

In a perfect world of money, there would be no booms or busts. The economy would grow enough each year to create just enough jobs to keep everyone happy. The supply of raw materials and finished goods would keep just ahead of the demand for those products. And salaries would rise in line with increases in consumer prices. But such a case of economic equilibrium rarely happens, if ever. Instead, the economy goes through a pattern of the good times and bad times.

Unfortunately, these economic cycles are hard both to diagnose and to predict. (This fact makes it easy for many economists to identify with the weather-predicting acumen of many meteorologists!) As if economic fluctuations didn't make an economist's job hard enough, the expansion of the nation's economy in recent years has resulted in regional differences in business conditions. For example, it is not unusual for some states to enjoy economic boom times while other states suffer in recession.

Boom times are characterized by above average growth in what economists call "gross domestic product," or "GDP." This figure, released quarterly by the U.S. Department of Commerce, tracks the growth of the value of all goods and services that the country produces. "Real GDP" reflects an adjustment to GDP growth by subtracting gains caused by inflation (price increases of goods and services). During this century real GDP has grown on average 3 percent a year.

Obviously, a growing economy is the preferred condition for most people. Sales boom, and in turn, companies create lots of new jobs. This leads to a demand for workers, which helps push up wages. The result is households that have more money to buy extra goods and services. Unfortunately, boom periods do not last forever.

When economic busts occur, real GDP becomes stagnant or decreases. Sales fall and companies cut jobs and wages. Unemployed workers, and those with smaller paychecks, must cut household expenditures. That results in even lower sales levels, forcing more companies to shutter factories and fire employees. It can become a vicious, downward spiral for the economy. Not all bust periods are recessions, though. A recession is classified by economists as an extended period of economic contraction. Depression is a diagnosis reserved for the rare, harsh collapse of the economy.

Recessions and depressions both have a political impact on the nation. President Bush lost the 1992 presidential election just a year after his leadership of victorious Allied forces in the Persian Gulf War. Political analysts say that Bush's defeat was due to the U.S. economy's painfully slow recovery from a recession. In fact, there is a great deal of political power that is associated with defining when the country is actually in recession. This is the main role of the National Bureau of Economic Research: It is a nonpartisan group of economists that serves as the official arbiters of a recession's start and end. As for the Bush recession, the bureau announced one month after Bill Clinton's victory in 1992 that the nation's ninth post–World War II recession officially began in July 1990 and ended in March 1991.

Three key forces create these boom and bust periods: external shocks, internal changes, and the nation's economic psyche.

Developments during the 1970s are a good example of how external forces can deal a blow to the economy. During that decade, an Arab-led oil embargo cut the supply of precious crude oil to the United States. As a result, the price of everything from gasoline to heating fuel to plastics made from petroleum soared. These higher prices sapped money from many corporate coffers and household budgets. As a result, purchases were curtailed and the nation's economy suffered through periods of recession or stagnation throughout much of the decade. Of course, an oil shortage wasn't bad news for all Americans. Those living in oil producing states—like Texas, Louisiana, Oklahoma, and Alaska—enjoyed prosperity because their crude oil was in high demand.

External shocks aren't always bad for the economy. While wars are never happy occurrences, the outbreak of fighting overseas usually starts an economic expansion. As the country gears up for war, the government's large buying binge for its troops allows many factories to run round-the-clock to manufacture the goods needed to fight a war. Of course, living through a wartime expansion can be difficult. During World War II, for example, many common goods become scarce as the military hoarded everything from rubber to wheat to keep the fighting forces both well-armed and well-fed.

The events of the 1980s illustrate how domestic policy decisions also play a role in creating booms and busts. Three key decisions helped create a climate that saw the longest boom since World War II: a huge tax cut; a large increase in defense spending; and the resulting growth in the national deficit.

The 1981 tax cut put more money in many Americans' checkbooks. A good portion of those tax savings was in turn spent on goods and services, creating a cycle of expansion for businesses and higher wages for employees. Higher wages boosted spending even further and helped fuel the decade's seven-year economic boom.

The huge defense buildup under President Reagan also boosted the 1980s economy, especially in the Northeastern United States and California, where many defense plants were. The government's call for more weapons, defensive systems, and troops meant more well-paid jobs for tens of thousands of people who worked both in and around the military. Spending by those workers added to the nationwide sales boom.

However, the government's tax revenues were never able to keep up with the military expenses. Congress and the president chose to run up huge deficits—borrowing to meet payrolls, bills, and other costs—rather than cutting back other parts of the government. That decision, too, helped the economy. It allowed people and companies who made money in and around the nonmilitary parts of U.S. government to keep spending and contributing to the economic expansion.

The deficit did catch up to the economy in the 1990s. When another tax cut could have helped the nation fully exit the 1990–1991 recession, Congress and President Bush were forced to impose a tax hike to help the government meet financial obligations. Economists say that this tax hike was one reason the economy was slow to recover from the recession. This economic slowdown likely cost President Bush a second term in the White House.

The nation's collective economic psyche also plays a big role in how booms and busts are created. The opinion of the nation's consumers on current business conditions is carefully watched, although it is often hard to measure it precisely. The University of Michigan, for example, does a monthly "consumer confidence" survey to see how average Americans feel about making big-ticket purchases. Other economists like to look at various measures of monthly sales at the nation's retailers for a snapshot of consumers' feeling about financial conditions. Economists are so interested in the consumer's view of the nation's economic health because consumers spend roughly two-thirds of all the money that flows through the country's economy.

This consumer sentiment is a powerful force. The end of the Persian Gulf War in January 1991 created a psychological lift that translated to a brief spending spree, creating enough of a boost from the purchases of automobiles, homes, refrigerators, and clothing that the 1990–1991 recession ended. However, the buying spree was short-lived. Few jobs were created by the early 1991 buying burst, and the economy stayed in a holding pattern until it was too late to help the Bush campaign.

How Economic Booms Create Inflation

Inflation is one of the key indications that the economy is growing. It represents a rise in prices for both raw materials and finished goods. Too much inflation, however, can be disruptive to many parts of the economy; it lowers the standard of living for many people, especially those living on fixed incomes. The U.S. Department of Labor uses the Consumer Price Index to track the cost of living; annual increases of more than 4 percent are seen as problematic. Here's a look at how inflation is created.

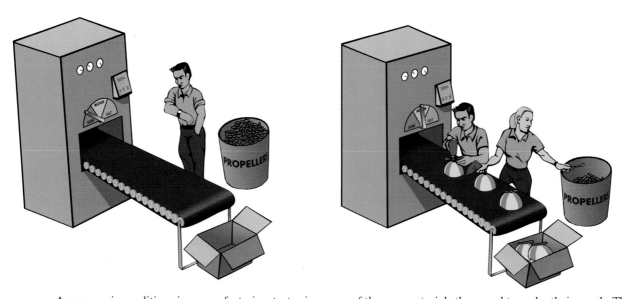

As economic conditions improve, factories start using more of the raw materials they need to make their goods. They begin rehiring previously laid-off workers or bring on new employees. This growth heightens the demand for raw materials and puts more money in consumers' checkbooks, allowing them to expand their purchases.

As economic growth continues, inflation can become problematic. Demand for more products means that raw materials and workers at the factories are in short supply. That forces factory managers to pay more for materials and wages. If the factory cannot pass on those increased costs to consumers, profits at the factory could be greatly impaired and workers' jobs could be imperiled.

A few key economic statistics are among the first to signal that renewed economic strength means inflation is growing. Here's a look at three of them.

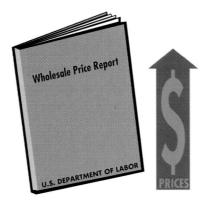

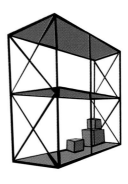

Factory Conditions

Once a month, the Federal Reserve Board issues its "Index of Industrial Production" reports on activity at manufacturers. During growth periods, the index will show increasing output and higher levels of the nation's total manufacturing capacity being used.

Commodity Prices

As factories begin to boost output, factory managers begin buying more raw materials. These purchases—or the anticipation of such purchases—help push up commodity prices. Every business day, investors trade commodity contracts in markets in New York and Chicago, which reflect these price trends. Also, once a month the Department of Labor issues its wholesale price report, which tracks price changes in goods used by manufacturers.

Warehouse Supplies

Does new economic growth result in companies stockpiling new products (not inflationary) or in dwindling inventories (inflationary)? So-called "inventory" economic indicators are released quarterly by the U.S. Department of Commerce and monthly by the National Association of Purchasing Managers. These are tricky numbers to decipher because it is not always clear if inventory shifts are due to changes in demand for goods or due to changes in inventory strategies.

Heavy inflation also hurts consumers. As more jobs are created, more families want various goods and services. But more potential buyers, and in some cases dwindling supplies, means that prices may rise sharply. If raises don't keep pace with the inflation rate, consumers end up losing buying power, and their standard of living actually falls despite the fatter paycheck.

How a Bankruptcy Works

A rise in the number of bankruptcy filings is one of the typical signs of an economic slump. By placing their own finances or a company under the protection of U.S. Bankruptcy Court, debtors get some breathing room from creditors such as landlords, lenders, or bill collectors. Successfully emerging from bankruptcy is no easy feat, as the bankruptcy obstacle course pushes roughly 90% of debtors into liquidation rather than a successful reorganization. Here's how a bankruptcy reorganization works.

A company or person has money problems. Debts are too high. They don't have any more cash to pay bills. Or they've lost a large legal judgment. Bankruptcy allows them to use the power of U.S. bankruptcy laws to negotiate settlement or repayment terms of their debts.

Sometimes, creditors act first. By filing an "involuntary bankruptcy petition," the creditors ask the court to protect their rights. These creditors typically fear that other parties are getting preferential payment treatment from the debtor while their bills go unpaid.

Various bankruptcy filings are specified by the U.S. Bankruptcy Code. Chapter 7 filing is a liquidation, a sale of assets to pay debts. Chapter 11 is a reorganization to let debtors rework their finances. Chapter 13 is for individuals, Chapter 12 is for farmers, and Chapter 9 is for local government bodies.

Bankruptcy law sets up a pecking order of who'll get repaid. "Secured" creditors (including loans backed by land, equipment, or inventory) and parties helping the debtor (attorneys, bankers, and so on) are paid first. "Unsecured" creditors (including personal lenders, suppliers, employees, bondholders, and taxes) get paid next. Shareholders are paid last.

A Chapter 11 reorganization gives the debtor 120 days to exclusively propose a plan to repay creditors; the deadline is often extended. The plan tells creditors and shareholders who will get what and projects who would be paid if the plan were to fail and the bankruptcy were converted to a Chapter 7 liquidation.

120 DAYS

SECURED CREDITORS

UNSECURED CREDITORS

DETOUR

Creditors can petition a bankruptcy judge to end the debtor's "exclusivity" and let creditors propose an alternative repayment plan. Usually one of the most influential groups in a bankruptcy reorganization is the creditors committee, which represents unsecured creditors with the most money at stake.

Whatever plan goes forward, that proposal must get the approval of a majority of the creditors. But all creditors are not created equal. The plan's authors can stack the votes in their favor by "classifying" various creditors—that is, giving certain creditors more voting power than others.

A bankruptcy judge gets the final say on a reorganization plan. Confirmation hearings are held, and these contentious proceedings can unravel a plan. If the judge, though, finds that a plan is in the best interests of creditors, he or she approves it, payments are made, and the bankruptcy ends.

AT THE BANK

CONTENTS

Chapter 7: Bank Accounts: A Family's Financial Backbone
44

Chapter 8: Interest Rates: The Price You Pay for Money
48

Chapter 9: Checking Accounts: Old and Reliable
54

Chapter 10: How ATMs Didn't Change the World
58

Chapter 11: Credit Cards: Plastic That Changed the World
62

Chapter 12: How the Loan Approval Process Works
66

Chapter 13: How Credit Reports Work
70

At one time, a banker was all that many Americans needed as far as financial services were concerned. The traditional banker worked at a commercial bank, savings and loan, or credit union—places that provided a safe place for a family's financial nest egg. The banker had products like checking accounts that could help a family make transactions. And often that same institution lent money to finance a home, car, college education, and so on.

The neighborhood bank was quite a profitable franchise for the banker. There were few competitors and the local bank enjoyed a lofty stature within American culture. Who can forget Jimmy Stewart playing small-town banker George Bailey in the Christmas-themed movie classic *It's a Wonderful Life*? By taking in deposits from fellow townspeople and then lending them out to others, Bailey saves the citizens of the mythical town of Bedford Falls from an evil, greedy banking competitor.

Times have changed dramatically for bankers, thanks to revamped regulations, modern technologies, new competitors, and new products. Furthermore, the notion that every American would need a traditional banker was once a given, but this thinking is now being challenged. In fact, some companies outside the banking industry may provide banking services, which confuses the banker's role in handling financial transactions.

Even the geography of the banking business is changing. At one time state lawmakers were very concerned about protecting the local nature of banking. In some states, that spirit helped create laws that limited bankers' ability to open new branches outside the county of origin. Other rules restricted banks from crossing state lines. But in 1994, new federal rules allow all U.S. bankers to open branches anywhere in the country.

The products offered by banks are changing, too. Once a simple passbook account kept track of your savings and the interest you were paid. Now traditional bankers offer everything from certificates of deposit with widely varying maturities and interest rates to uninsured investments—like money market mutual funds (pools of money invested in conservative interest-paying notes), or "annuities" (life insurance products that pay interest and have some tax advantages). But these uninsured products are just copies of what other financial companies have been successfully selling for years.

Now consider the checking account, a banking mainstay for households to pay bills. Today, bankers can pay you interest on your checking balance, and you can get a checking account at almost any bank, savings and loan, or credit union. But stock brokerages and mutual fund companies offer accounts with checking privileges, too.

Bankers' lock on lending has also been chipped away. Once savings and loans were the major force in lending for home purchases. Now, huge so-called "mortgage bankers" like Countrywide Funding of California, lead the pack. Mortgage bankers typically use private investors' funds, rather than deposits, to make home loans. The credit card business, popularized by California's Bank of America and dominated by New York's Citibank, is now facing stiff challenges from products linked to communications giant AT&T and to the world's largest carmaker, General Motors. And when it comes to car loans, the major automakers' own finance companies are the bankers behind about half the new vehicle financing in America. And if an automaker isn't lending the money for a new car, there's a good chance that another nontraditional lender will make the loan: the industrial conglomerate General Electric's finance business.

Bankers' modern twists contend with serious competition. Automated teller machines, those 24-hour banking machines, have drawn a loyal following. They make it easy to get cash (or these days, things like stamps and travelers checks) both at bank branches and at busy spots like airports and shopping malls. But one of the fastest growing operators of teller machines in the early 1990s isn't a bank, it's Electronic Data Systems. The Texas-based company is targeting convenience stores for its teller machine business.

With all the product competition, there is still one distinguishing trait that bankers control today. That's the sale of federally insured deposit accounts. Put up to $100,000 in a bank, savings and loan, or credit union, and that money is guaranteed by the U.S. government, no matter what happens to that banking institution. Don't let anyone sway you into thinking that federal deposit insurance isn't rock solid.

Evidence mounts, however, that consumers are very confused about bankers' new products. Many bankers have responded to competitive pressures by increasing their own investment-selling activities. This has confounded many savers. Several surveys in 1993 and 1994 by both government and private groups found that the public generally did not know that banker-sold investments in stocks, bonds, mutual funds, or life insurance did not carry protection by the U.S. government.

It was such misunderstandings that gave Arizona businessman Charles Keating, Jr., the opportunity to sell 13,000 Southern California investors $200 million in what proved to be worthless investments. Assuming the cloak of safety associated with bankers' offices, the 13,000 mainly elderly savers at Keating's Lincoln Savings and Loan were convinced to switch their insured savings accounts to IOUs from Keating's business empire. When Keating's S&L and others businesses went broke in 1989, the elderly savers' uninsured investments became worthless. Meanwhile, U.S. taxpayers paid more than $3 billion to insure that all of Lincoln S&L's savings accounts were protected from any loss.

CHAPTER
7

Bank Accounts: A Family's Financial Backbone

NO FINANCIAL PRODUCT reaches more Americans than the ubiquitous bank account. Approximately seven out of every eight households have some basic savings relationship with a bank, savings and loan, or credit union. The bank account—often called a "savings account"—serves as the backbone for a family's finances. These accounts are a place to store spare money safely while earning a modest interest rate. "Liquidity"—the ability to quickly get at invested money—is typically not a high priority for savings accounts. In contrast, checking accounts used to pay bills and other obligations offer greater liquidity. All of the bank accounts discussed in this chapter are backed by federal deposit insurance, except for money funds.

Over the years, the savings account has evolved through technology and marketing. A century ago, savings account balances were kept by bankers, who made entries in paper ledgers at the bank offices. The 20th century brought the "passbook account," for which each deposit and withdrawal was stamped into a saver's passbook (much like a traveler's passport is stamped). In the 1980s, passbooks gave way to "statement accounts" or "money market accounts," where savers got a receipt with each transaction and a complete record ("statement") of their dealings mailed to their home each month. At the same time, automated teller machines gave round-the-clock access to cash in many money market accounts.

Today, bankers offer savers several alternatives to the plain savings account.

Short-term CDs (certificates of deposits), with maturities of 30 to 120 days, can offer slightly higher interest rates than savings accounts. However, savers can be penalized for "early withdrawal"—taking money out before the maturity date.

Checking accounts that pay interest keep savings very liquid and pay interest on money until you need to spend it. These accounts often have hefty monthly fees that can more than wipe out any interest payments. For savers to avoid these fees, many bankers require sizable minimum balances. That ties up some savings to make these accounts a profitable choice for consumers.

The latest wrinkle is money market mutual funds, or simply "money funds." These accounts work much like regular money market accounts, but they carry no federal deposit insurance. Their safety comes from pooling investors' money and buying very liquid, very secure short-term interest-bearing investments. But remember, there are no guarantees.

How a Bank Transaction Is Recorded

Making a deposit, withdrawal, or loan payment at a bank seems like a simple process. But to ensure both the safety of the bank's money, and the integrity of your account, bankers typically use a complex routine to record every transaction. In this example you'll deposit $500 in cash and a check for $1,000 into your savings account.

1 You give the teller the cash, the check, and a deposit slip. In return, you get a receipt that details the transaction. The receipt is a record of the dollar amount involved, the teller, the branch, and so forth. It's very handy to keep in case problems ever arise.

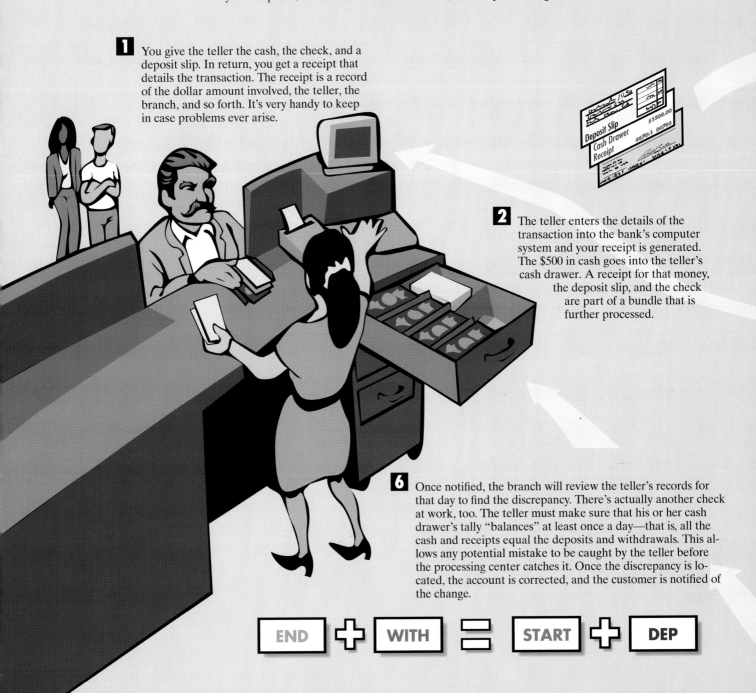

2 The teller enters the details of the transaction into the bank's computer system and your receipt is generated. The $500 in cash goes into the teller's cash drawer. A receipt for that money, the deposit slip, and the check are part of a bundle that is further processed.

6 Once notified, the branch will review the teller's records for that day to find the discrepancy. There's actually another check at work, too. The teller must make sure that his or her cash drawer's tally "balances" at least once a day—that is, all the cash and receipts equal the deposits and withdrawals. This allows any potential mistake to be caught by the teller before the processing center catches it. Once the discrepancy is located, the account is corrected, and the customer is notified of the change.

END ✚ WITH ═ START ✚ DEP

3 All teller bundles are collected at least once a day from all bank branches and taken to a central processing center. This is a relatively new method in banking. Before, the paperwork of each branch was double-checked and processed on site in the so-called "back shop."

4 At the processing center, every document is first microfilmed. This allows bankers to keep records of every transaction for years. Then the details of the transaction are entered for a second time into the bankers' computer system.

5 The computer now checks the teller's entry against the processing center's entry for your $1,500 deposit. If everything matches, the transaction is recorded. If not, the transaction is flagged and the branch is contacted.

STATEMENT

ACCT: 9876 543210

Mr. and Mrs. John Norway
1000 Easy St.
Mountain Top, USA

October 6, 1994

CHAPTER
8

Interest Rates: The Price You Pay for Money

NTEREST RATES AREN'T numbers pulled out of the air by cheap bankers (on deposits) or greedy lenders (on loans.) Actually, there's a science behind interest rates that might be best called "the price of money."

The system that determines interest rates works as it does in any other marketplace, from the corner grocery store to the world's financial exchanges. Interest rates are typically determined by the interaction between the amount of money that a seller (typically a lender or investor) demands and an amount a buyer (typically a borrower) can afford to pay for money to change hands for a specified amount of time. (For example, when you go to the bank to open a savings account, you're the seller and the banker is the buyer who is borrowing money from you!)

Economic theory holds that the key bargaining point between the sellers and buyers of money in determining interest rates is the expectation of future inflation. Inflation is usually defined as the rise or fall of consumer prices; it is the enemy of any person or institution giving up the use of their money in exchange for a fixed rate of interest. For example, imagine lending $10,000 at 4 percent interest rate for a year. So, at the end of the loan, you will get $10,400 back. That sounds pretty good at first, right? But say in those previous 12 months, inflation rises by 6 percent. That amount of inflation makes what cost $10,000 a year earlier cost $10,600 when the loan is paid. This means you or the lender in this case actually will lose $200 worth of buying power in a year. Obviously, you should have asked for at least 6 percent just to stay even with inflation. In fact, if you or any lender knew that inflation was going to be 6 percent, you would likely demand an interest rate above 6 percent, so you could end up with what economists call a *real profit*—that is, money made in excess of the inflation rate.

Now, in our example, our lender made a one-year mistake. Imagine making a five-year mistake? Or a 20-year mistake? Ouch! It is obvious that people lending their money to others for long periods of time have a very hard time guessing what inflation rates will be well into the future. Typically, long-term lenders demand an interest rate well above the current rate of inflation (or the prevailing estimates of what the inflation rate will be). This higher interest rate serves as insurance for the lender in case the return fails to keep up with the inflation rate.

The inflation factor explains why in normal economic climates long-term interest rates—whether they be on savings or borrowings—are higher than interest rates for short-term money. However, interest rates aren't always that simple nor do inflation rates alone always determine the price of money.

Let's look at the cost of providing money to someone to better understand how interest rates are calculated. For example, a lender who services mortgages has few operating costs. One cost is collecting payments from borrowers. The other major cost for a lender would be defaults where borrowers no longer make payments and eventually lose their houses through foreclosure. This is a relatively rare event and barely figures in the mortgage's interest rate calculation. Due to low servicing costs and equally low foreclosure-loss costs, fixed-rate mortgages can be obtained for less than 1 percentage point above the prevailing 15-year or 30-year U.S. Treasury bond interest rate.

Now let's look at the costs associated with providing credit cards to consumers. The credit card company has numerous costs. First, there are the roughly four out of ten "convenience" cardholders who pay off their entire charge card balance every month to avoid paying any interest. The card company has to bear the cost of losing the use of their money for as long as 60 days because they paid the merchant immediately after goods were purchased. Next is the heavy cost of tabulating all the purchases made by a cardholder in a month and sending out a bill. Then, on top of these costs are the high costs of credit card fraud (where cards are stolen) and defaults by cardholders who cannot afford what they have purchased. Add these up and you'll understand why credit cards' annual interest rates run between 6 and 15 percentage points above the card companies' raw cost for money.

Another factor in determinating interest rates is the demand for money. Consider a neighborhood where two or three new bank branches have opened. It's just like when new competing supermarkets come to town. Each new branch manager has to quickly bring in new business, such as loans and deposits. And just as a grocer offers weekly specials on food or dry goods, a banker may try to beat the competition and get your money by offering higher than normal interest rates on savings accounts. Or, the banker will entice you to borrow money with lower than normal rates on loans.

Now, let's take a look at the demand for money on a broader, national scale. In the middle of the 1980s, the U.S. economy was booming. Businesses were building new factories and new office buildings, and consumers wanted new cars and homes.

Everyone, it seemed, wanted a loan. That meant that bankers could keep the interest rates on loans high.

However, in the heat of the borrowing frenzy of the late 1980s, bankers fought for money to lend. In turn, that demand pushed interest rates offered on savings accounts at some banks and S&Ls approximately 3 full percentage points above the similar Treasury bonds. Conversely, in 1992 and 1993 the U.S. economy was acting poorly and banks and savings and loans (S&Ls) found few businesspersons or consumers wanting to borrow. Bankers had little need for cash to lend. As a result, interest rates on savings accounts fell to 1 percentage point or more below the similar Treasury bond interest rates.

One way to track interest rates on bank and S&L accounts is to look at a comparable rate on a U.S. Treasury bond. Both savings accounts and "Treasuries" (as they are called by traders) carry the insurance of repayment by the U.S. government, making them very safe investments. And because interest rates on Treasuries are derived from a world's worth of traders competing for them every business day, Treasuries are seen as a good benchmarks for investors to compare interest rates. In an ordinary economic situation, interest rates on bank and S&L accounts should roughly equal a similar Treasury bond. (For example, a one-year CD should earn about the same as a one-year Treasury.)

Where Interest Rates Come From

Broad moves on the interest rate roller coaster are directly tied to inflation, which is a measure of the changes in consumer prices. The graph below shows how the interest rate on a one-year U.S. Treasury bill has roughly mimicked the annual change in consumer prices over the last two decades. It was compiled from figures from *Bloomberg Business News* in New York.

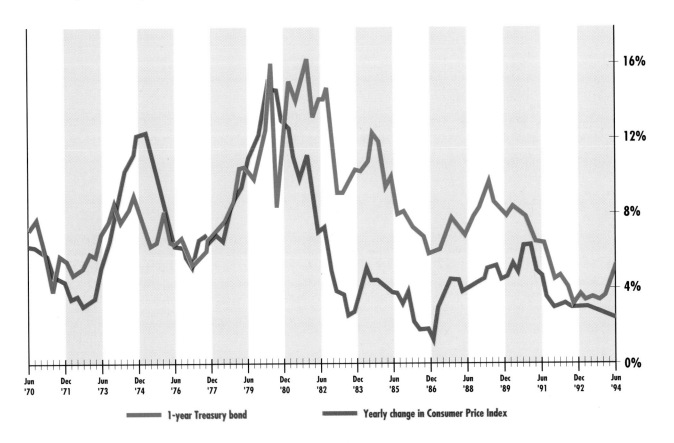

■■■■ 1-year Treasury bond   **■■■■ Yearly change in Consumer Price Index**

You can't look at just one interest rate to find out what's happening to the interest rates that affect your life. This is because various financial products are tied to interest rates of differing maturity; these rates move somewhat independently of each other. Consider the three graphs to the right, known to traders as "yield curves." The yield curve shows interest rates on U.S. Treasury bonds of various key maturities at the last three presidential inaugurations and lists what consumer products are affected by those rates. The figures for these graphs were compiled from *Bloomberg Business News*.

Shortest-term rates   Interest rates on U.S. Treasury bonds with maturities of under 1 year (often called T-bills) serve as the base for many consumer-related interest rates: savings accounts; interest-bearing checking accounts; money market mutual funds; variable-rate credit cards; and many adjustable home loans.

Short-term rates   Interest rates on U.S. Treasury bonds of one year to three years in maturity serve as guideposts for interest rates on the following: 1-to-3 year certificates of deposit (CDs); guaranteed or "steady-value" insurance contracts; and some adjustable home mortgages.

Intermediate-term rates   Interest rates on U.S. Treasury bonds of three years to ten years in maturity serve as guideposts to set interest rates on automobile loans; U.S. Savings Bonds; long-term CDs; and some hybrid (part-fixed, part-adjustable) mortgages.

Long-term rates   There's only one major consumer-related financial item whose interest rate is tied to interest rates on U.S. Treasury bonds of 10 years to 30 years: that is fixed-rate, long-term mortgages.

January 20, 1985: Ronald Reagan was sworn in for his second term as president. Note the traditional slope of the yield curve from low short-term rates to higher, long-term rates.

January 20, 1989: When George Bush was sworn in, there was a rare "inverted yield curve" position, with most short-term interest rates above the rates on longer maturities. This foreshadowed future economic problems.

January 20, 1993: Bill Clinton's inauguration came at a time that the Federal Reserve was pushing short-term interest rates lower in an attempt to stimulate an ailing U.S. economy.

Checking Accounts: Old and Reliable

THE CHECKING ACCOUNT is a traditional payment method used by most households. A check represents an order from a check writer to a banker to draw a specified amount from the writer's account to pay the party listed on the check.

Crude versions of checks existed in early Rome, and checks became a common form of payment in 16th and 17th century Europe. However, primitive check systems required the recipient of a check to personally go to the check writer's bank to collect the money. As commerce spread around the globe, that practice became impractical. Soon bankers were providing "clearing" services to those who received checks which allowed them to collect payment. These clearing services evolved into central clearinghouses, where bankers would meet to exchange checks and money to make those checks good. In the United States, the establishment of a national check clearinghouse was a key reason Congress established the nation's central bank, the Federal Reserve System, in 1913.

If the pundits of the 1970s had been right, checks would just be part of a history lesson today. They predicted a technology revolution that would include services that can transmit funds electronically. While such payment systems are available to the average consumer, their use is still not as widespread as anticipated. So throughout the 1980s and early 1990s, the volume of checks written in the United States grew slightly though steadily.

Checks have survived for several reasons. Of course, there is technophobia, the fear that has slowed broad adoption of many 20th century inventions, such as electronic payment systems. Another consumer appeal of the old paper-based payment process is the built-in receipt: the reassurance received from a canceled check from the bank. Checking also is an inexpensive way to move money. Outside of new systems that pay vast numbers of bills, no electronic payment service has emerged that can beat the modest expenses of buying printed checks and mailing them.

The checking account has benefited from marketing. Savings and loans and credit unions, prohibited from offering checking accounts until the 1980s, now compete with commercial bankers for these prized customers. Also, interest may be paid on idle balances. Even the traditional "safety blue" check paper is passé: Designs of individual checks now range from landscapes to imprints of Elvis Presley. And if you need cash instantly from your checking account, automated teller machines give you 24-hour access to your money.

How the Check Clearing System Works

Here's a look at how the nation's clearing system actually gets your bills paid, makes sure the correct amount is taken from your checking account, and sees to it that the check is returned to you. Bankers and check processors use everything from trucks to private cargo flights to swiftly move checks around the globe.

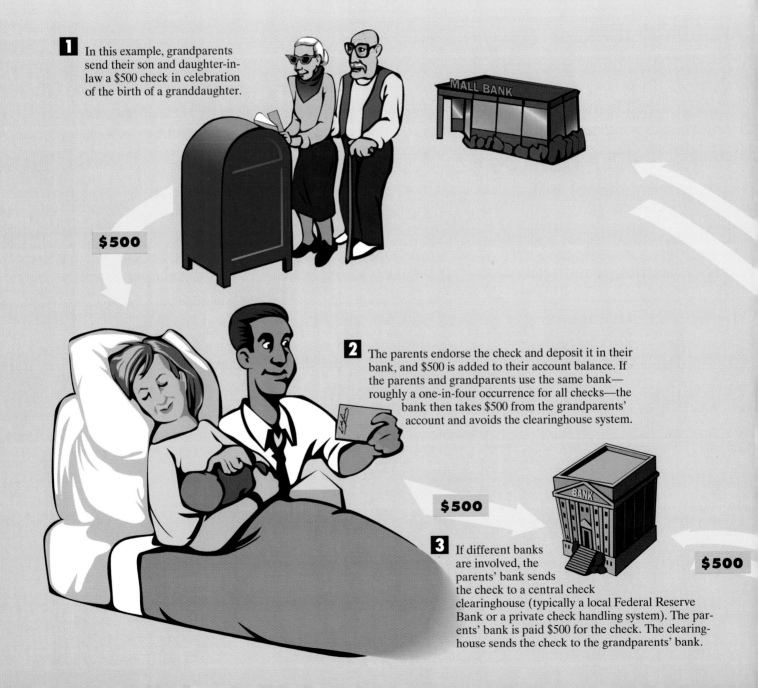

1 In this example, grandparents send their son and daughter-in-law a $500 check in celebration of the birth of a granddaughter.

$500

MALL BANK

2 The parents endorse the check and deposit it in their bank, and $500 is added to their account balance. If the parents and grandparents use the same bank—roughly a one-in-four occurrence for all checks—the bank then takes $500 from the grandparents' account and avoids the clearinghouse system.

$500

BANK

3 If different banks are involved, the parents' bank sends the check to a central check clearinghouse (typically a local Federal Reserve Bank or a private check handling system). The parents' bank is paid $500 for the check. The clearinghouse sends the check to the grandparents' bank.

$500

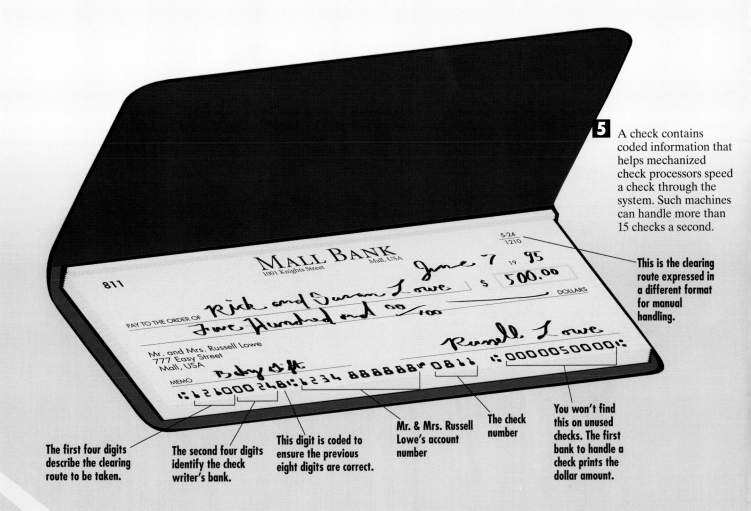

5 A check contains coded information that helps mechanized check processors speed a check through the system. Such machines can handle more than 15 checks a second.

This is the clearing route expressed in a different format for manual handling.

The first four digits describe the clearing route to be taken.

The second four digits identify the check writer's bank.

This digit is coded to ensure the previous eight digits are correct.

Mr. & Mrs. Russell Lowe's account number

The check number

You won't find this on unused checks. The first bank to handle a check prints the dollar amount.

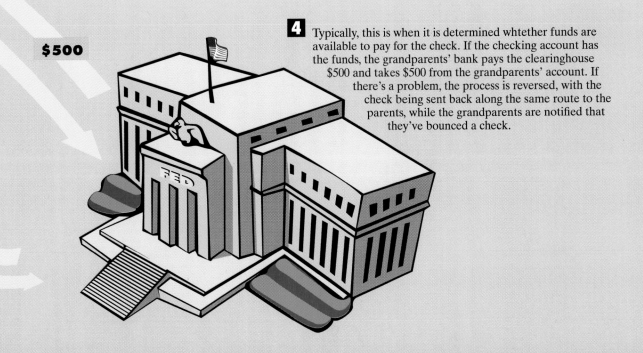

$500

4 Typically, this is when it is determined whtether funds are available to pay for the check. If the checking account has the funds, the grandparents' bank pays the clearinghouse $500 and takes $500 from the grandparents' account. If there's a problem, the process is reversed, with the check being sent back along the same route to the parents, while the grandparents are notified that they've bounced a check.

How ATMs Didn't Change the World

N 1971, THE automated teller machine (ATM) entered the American banking landscape when the first mechanized cash dispenser and deposit taker was installed at a bank in San Bernardino, California. ATMs give 24-hour availability of basic banking services to customers who get access to their accounts with a "bank card," or "ATM card," and a personal code called a "PIN" (personal identification number).

By the late 1970s, some banking experts were suggesting that ATMs would eventually make the bank branch an endangered species. Bankers began to dream of the day they could use an ATM network to rid themselves of expensive offices and branch employees. Other experts proclaimed that the bank card would help lead America to the "cashless society," where consumers used electronic banking services, rather than currency or checks.

What bankers have learned, however, is that the public isn't quite ready for full-scale automated banking. Many customers, notably older ones, are fearful of the new technology. Other people are scared to make deposits at ATMs for security reasons. And some say they prefer the occasional visit to the bank branch to a transaction with a cold, impersonal machine. Still, there's enough interest in electronic banking that in 1993 there was one ATM for every 25,000 Americans, according to the Bank Network News newsletter.

Those who have adapted to ATMs over the years have followed the increasing versatility of this technology. ATMs are no longer located just at branch sites. They can be found in shopping malls and airports, at retailers from supermarkets to convenience stores, and even in gambling casinos. And ATMs are no longer just for dispensing cash and making deposits. Bankers have outfitted their machines to do various new chores. They can sell stamps, bus tickets, and travelers checks; allow investors to switch money between bank-sold investment accounts; and generate detailed mini-statements of recent banking activities.

To further contribute to this flexibility, a consumer can use a bank card to get cash at numerous institutions other than his or her own bank, thanks to electronic networks of banking institutions. Consumers who don't like the idea of using credit cards for routine purchases can still shop with plastic at "point-of-sale" (POS) terminals. At a POS, you use your bank card to buy everything from gasoline to groceries to fast food to goods at major retailers. And many of these same merchants will advance consumers extra cash with their purchase from the bank card if they so desire.

How Bank Cards Work

Did you know that the average bank card is used twice as frequently as the average general-purpose credit card? Here's a look at how automated teller machines (ATMs) and bank cards work together to give consumers easy global access to the funds in their bank accounts.

The key to this global reach is the growth of major ATM networks—such as Star, MAC, NYCE, Honor, Cirrus, and Maestro. These groups link banks with their account databases, allowing transactions to occur instantly. Here's how a network lets you use your bank card to bank and buy at thousands of places around the world.

The traditional bank ATM dispenses cash and accepts deposits if the machine is owned by your bank. Bankers consider ATM deposits more secure than transactions with a teller because two bank officers unload and check all deposits made at an ATM.

Many retailers, from merchandisers to restaurants, now accept bank cards for payment. These "point-of-sale" (POS) terminals at a checkout counter work much like an ATM.

Cash dispensers, physically smaller and limited-function ATMs, are now frequently placed in high-traffic locations such as airports and retailers' lobbies.

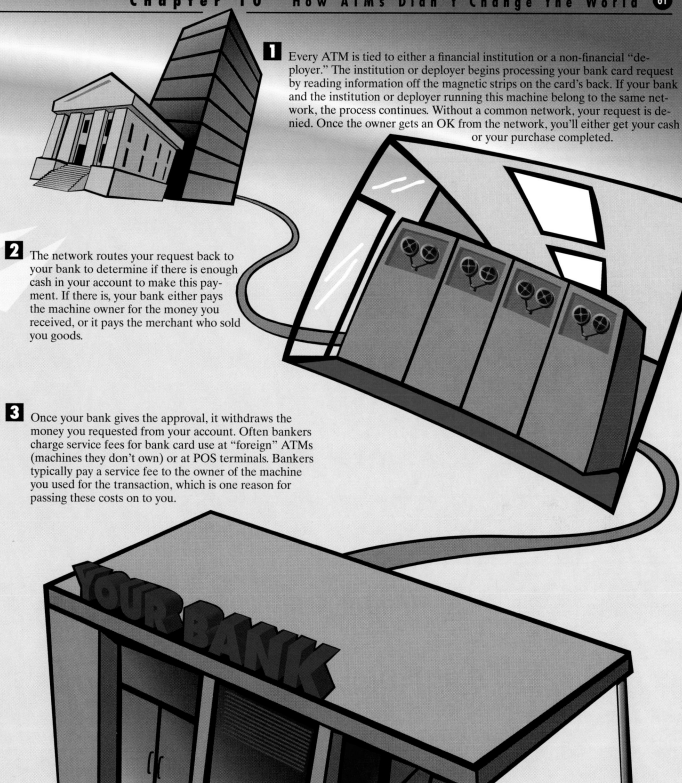

1 Every ATM is tied to either a financial institution or a non-financial "deployer." The institution or deployer begins processing your bank card request by reading information off the magnetic strips on the card's back. If your bank and the institution or deployer running this machine belong to the same network, the process continues. Without a common network, your request is denied. Once the owner gets an OK from the network, you'll either get your cash or your purchase completed.

2 The network routes your request back to your bank to determine if there is enough cash in your account to make this payment. If there is, your bank either pays the machine owner for the money you received, or it pays the merchant who sold you goods.

3 Once your bank gives the approval, it withdraws the money you requested from your account. Often bankers charge service fees for bank card use at "foreign" ATMs (machines they don't own) or at POS terminals. Bankers typically pay a service fee to the owner of the machine you used for the transaction, which is one reason for passing these costs on to you.

STATEMENT

ACCT: 9876 543210

October 1, 1995

WITHDRAWAL: FarAway S+L $100.00
Non-Your Bank ATM Service Charge $2.00

Credit Cards: Plastic That Changed the World

NO FINANCIAL PRODUCT has brought greater change to the spending habits of Americans than the general-purpose credit card. Credit cards are unsecured lines of credit that function as personal loans of varying amounts that the customer determines. They allow consumers to use plastic identification cards, instead of cash or checks, to buy goods and services from numerous merchants worldwide.

The roots of this service date to the start of the 20th century. Many hotels, department stores, and gasoline companies began to offer "charge cards." Unlike the modern credit card, these accounts only allowed a consumer to buy products at the sponsoring merchant, and bills were payable upon receipt, so there was no extension of credit.

It wasn't until 1949, with the start of the Diners Club card that targeted restaurant customers, that consumers could use the same charge card at different places. In the 1950s, bankers' first general-purpose credit cards were limited to use in the same state as the issuing bank. But in 1966, the modern general-purpose credit card came of age: San Francisco-based Bank of America took its BankAmericard (the forerunner of today's Visa card) nationwide.

Today, these general-purpose cards pay for roughly $1 of every $10 spent by Americans. The cards serve as the third most popular way to borrow—behind mortgages and car loans. The card industry is dominated by three brands: Visa and MasterCard, both issued by financial institutions, and the proprietary American Express card.

Credit cards have been a boon to many consumers. For those who pay off their balances each month, cards provide interest-free credit from the time of purchase until the bill is due. The cards have spurred the growth of businesses such as mail-order retailing and car rentals. By allowing the choice of borrowing, these cards can help a family's cash flow as they extend to the family flexible credit once reserved for the wealthy. The cards also provide a sense of security by enabling many emergency expenses—from car repairs to hospital visits—to be instantly met.

But credit cards have a dark side, too. Fraudulent use, through stolen cards or account numbers, is a billion-dollar-a-year business. Millions of consumers have overspent with credit cards, creating financial woes including personal bankruptcies. And critics claim that many card-issuing bankers have kept fees and interest rates unusually high, producing windfall profits.

How the Credit Card System Works

Thanks to modern computing and communications power, a consumer can use a general-purpose credit card to easily pay for goods and services at merchants around the globe. Here's an example of how the Visa and MasterCard system works:

1 The issuing bank agrees to give the consumer a credit card with a specified spending limit. The consumer is free to use that card at any merchant accepting that brand of card around the globe.

2 Our consumer spends $50 on a gift and tells the merchant that a credit card will be used to pay for the item.

3 The merchant is able to accept credit card purchases because he or she established a relationship with a "merchant bank" that handles credit card transactions. The merchant must verify that our consumer's card is valid, so the merchant typically uses a direct communications link to ask the merchant bank for approval of the charge.

4 The merchant bank checks electronically with the credit card network's databases to see if our consumer's card is good and that there's sufficient credit remaining. If everything checks out, the $50 charge is approved and the merchant is paid (less a servicing fee of 1% to 6%) by the merchant bank.

$50

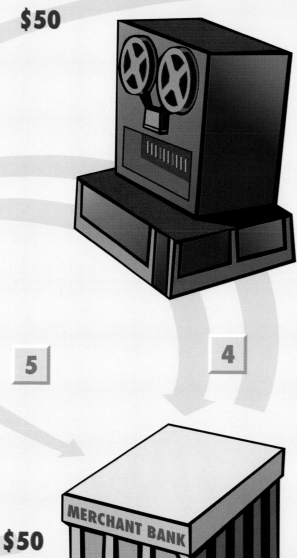

5 Using the same credit card network, the merchant bank asks our consumer's issuing bank to pay for the charge. The issuing bank pays the merchant bank $50, less a service fee (typically 1% to 2%).

6 The issuing bank tallies all our consumer's card purchases once a month and sends a bill by mail. The consumer now can choose to either pay the balance or make a minimum payment and borrow ("revolve," as a banker might say) the rest.

Inside a Card Deal

Remember, each issuing bank offers different terms. Consumers will find that card pricing varies greatly, including cases where the same bank offers multiple cards with dissimilar terms. Here's a look at some key questions to ask when shopping for a card:

Interest Rate: What rate is charged on purchases? Or when borrowing money, what rate is charged on "cash advances"? How is the balance determined on which interest is charged?

Time: What's the "grace period" between when a bill is mailed and when payment is due? "No grace" cards always accrue interest charges.

Fees: Any annual fee for use of the card? For late payments? For exceeding the predetermined credit limit?

Credit Limits: How much can you spend with this card? What about cash advances? Can you raise these limits?

Other: Is a toll-free telephone hot line offered? Is it staffed round-the-clock? Are there additional services or rebate programs?

How the Loan Approval Process Works

LOAN APPROVAL IS a decision-making process that's part science and part art. Many loans, up to the amount needed to buy a car, are typically done by computer analysis of your application and credit history. In many cases, approvals are made almost instantly, unless there is a problem or an unusual case. Then, a lender personally intercedes. Bigger loans, such as real estate and small business lending, require the human touch (and a lot more paperwork) to determine the creditworthiness of a loan applicant.

One misconception of banking is that the only people who seem to get loans are the ones who don't need the money. While that may seem to be the case, more loans are available to a broad spectrum of people in the United States than anywhere else in the world.

To understand why loans appear to be so hard to get, you have to understand what is at stake. For lenders to make money giving out loans, they first must find cheap sources of funds, typically from depositors or investors. Then the lenders grant loans that pay them interest greater than the interest paid to those sources of loan money *plus* the expense of making and maintaining the loan. Losses from late or deadbeat borrowers can throw the lender's profit equation out of kilter. Few lenders can profit by selling off repossessed cars or homes. For example, credit card lenders typically get back 2¢ for each $1 lent to someone who goes bankrupt.

It's the risk of loss that makes the loan application process so detailed. By collecting piles of data about you, the lender is trying to figure out if you'll pay them back. That's why successful borrowers continue to get more loans. It's also why people with bad credit find it difficult to regain lenders' confidence.

Lenders have not had the best reputation, however, of being fair in their loan approvals. Some of this is explained by lenders' slow adaptation to societal changes. For instance, it wasn't until the mid-1970s that both a husband and wife's income were regularly used to qualify for loans. It was previously assumed by lenders that the woman would eventually stop working to raise the family's children. Furthermore, several national studies of home mortgages showed that nonwhites are turned down more frequently than whites, even when household income is equal. In the 1990s, some lenders are now allowing three or more incomes to be used to qualify for a mortgage. This allows many multiple-income households to use collective incomes to qualify to buy that home.

Loan Approval: A Juggling Act

Lenders juggle many variables when it comes to deciding who gets loans and who doesn't. Here's what bankers are looking for in applications and interviews. Also take a look at what they find out from their own loan departments and reports from credit bureaus.

Character

Personal traits of the applicant are important, especially in bigger loans for cars, homes, and small businesses. Lenders like to see a borrower who is a long-time resident of the region, especially one who has lived in the same home for several years. They prefer applicants who have had the same employer for years. But there's flexibility if there are good reasons for moves or job changes. The character issue is why it's important to be honest about finances and previous problems.

Collateral

The lender wants to know how they're protected if there's trouble with a loan. "Collateral" is what backs up the loan (a home in a mortgage, the car in a car loan, inventory in a small business loan). For a mortgage, the lender will likely have the home appraised to check its value. The down payment, also called "equity," is what the borrower has at stake. The greater the down payment, the better lenders feel. And while low down payment mortgages are available, they typically require applicants with near-perfect credit records.

Application

Fill out this form as completely and accurately as possible. Don't be afraid to disclose any previous payment problems, because it's likely the lender will discover them later when they contact credit bureaus. Lenders like honesty and will respond positively in follow-up interviews to stories of how you worked out of previous credit problems. Remember that lying to a lender on a loan application is a crime.

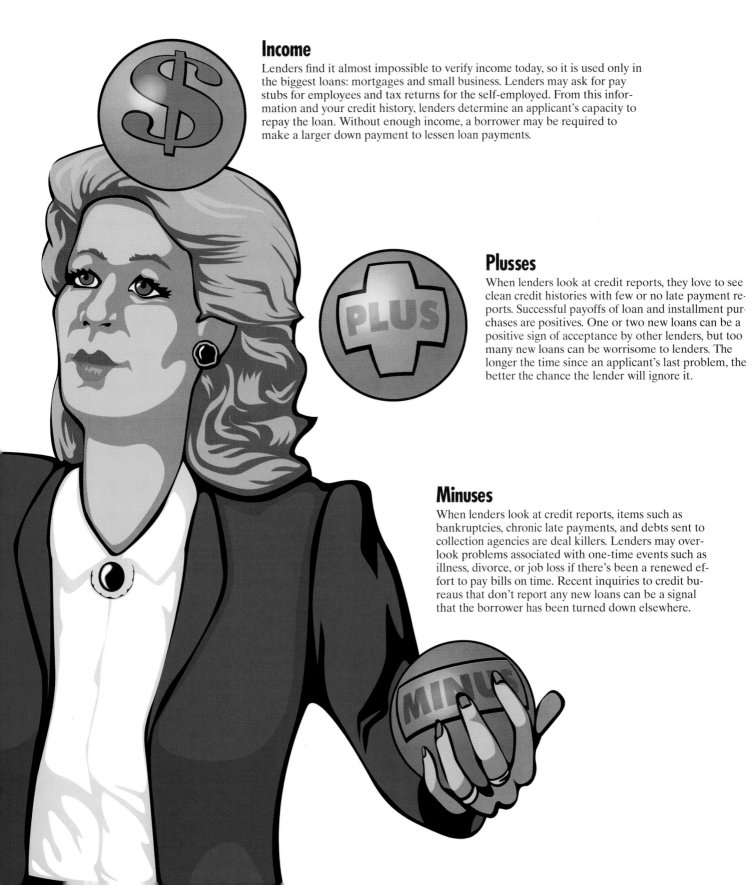

Income

Lenders find it almost impossible to verify income today, so it is used only in the biggest loans: mortgages and small business. Lenders may ask for pay stubs for employees and tax returns for the self-employed. From this information and your credit history, lenders determine an applicant's capacity to repay the loan. Without enough income, a borrower may be required to make a larger down payment to lessen loan payments.

Plusses

When lenders look at credit reports, they love to see clean credit histories with few or no late payment reports. Successful payoffs of loan and installment purchases are positives. One or two new loans can be a positive sign of acceptance by other lenders, but too many new loans can be worrisome to lenders. The longer the time since an applicant's last problem, the better the chance the lender will ignore it.

Minuses

When lenders look at credit reports, items such as bankruptcies, chronic late payments, and debts sent to collection agencies are deal killers. Lenders may overlook problems associated with one-time events such as illness, divorce, or job loss if there's been a renewed effort to pay bills on time. Recent inquiries to credit bureaus that don't report any new loans can be a signal that the borrower has been turned down elsewhere.

How Credit Reports Work

A "CREDIT REPORT" is a history of your bill paying and borrowing. A private data collection company known as a "credit bureau" compiles the report. Lenders, landlords, and others who want to do business with you use your credit history to estimate your ability to repay them.

Before the computer age, credit bureaus were mainly regional businesses that kept paper records of your payment history. Reports from local bankers and merchants were placed in your credit-history folder. This time-consuming process limited your borrowing ability primarily to the region where you lived. Electronic data storage helped create nationwide credit bureaus. Today, three companies dominate the credit reporting business: TRW, Equifax, and Trans Union. They oversee credit histories of more than 180 million Americans.

While having a company keep a detailed history of your bill paying may seem unnerving, the system is actually quite beneficial. Credit bureaus do not approve loan applications. Rather, by providing a wealth of credit data in minutes, credit bureaus give the typical American unparalleled access to loans. With just one telephone call, many merchants can get enough information from a credit bureau to sell big appliances and automobiles on instant credit. The same system allows a family to quickly buy a new house after relocating across the country. Only wealthy consumers commonly enjoy such service elsewhere in the world.

Credit bureaus, though, have been the source of problems. For example, consumers might learn of errors in their credit histories. But for years consumers complained that it was very difficult to get those errors removed. During the early 1990s, a series of government actions made it easier for consumers to keep their credit histories correct. It's a good habit to regularly check your credit history. This can be done inexpensively. Call the major bureaus (TRW at (800) 422-4879; Equifax at (800) 685-1111; Trans Union at (312) 258-1717) for details.

If you have a bad credit history, however, there is little you can do to alter the bureaus' records. Con artists have made millions selling credit repair services that offer illegal or ineffective cures. The best advice if you have bad credit is to get a copy of your credit report; make sure the negative items are correct; and make sure that positive credit activities are on the report, too. Then begin paying debts on time. Try a "secured" credit card (backed by a deposit at the lending institution) and use it wisely. It may take years, but you can become a good credit risk again.

Inside a Credit Report

Here's a look at how major credit bureaus compile your credit history and what's contained in your credit report.

Public Documents

The bureaus search court and other public records for information about legal judgments, liens, bankruptcies, and other problematic actions. These are added to your credit history.

Applications

One major source for a credit history are loan applications you fill out. This information is passed to bureaus for verification and may reveal information the bureau was unaware of.

Creditor Updates

Merchants and creditors constantly feed the bureaus with a history of credit extended and your payment history. This includes both positive and negative payment news.

Consumer Feedback

You can help your credit history by informing bureaus of inaccuracies. Corrected mistakes on the credit history are typically shared among the three major bureaus.

CREDIT REPORT

APPLICATIONS

PUBLIC DOCUMENTS

CREDITOR UPDATES

CONSUMER FEEDBACK

The three major credit bureaus' credit history reports are designed quite differently. But each contains the following types of data that are used to puzzle together your application.

Personal Information

Two types: Current information including name, address, and Social Security number; other identifiers such as year of birth, spouse's name, previous residences, employers, and/or nicknames.

Credit History

Three key elements: Listing of merchant or creditor and account; description of that financial arrangement; and a status report on payment history and outstanding liabilities.

Other Items

Two key areas: A list of who has looked at your credit history recently and why; and contact information detailing how you can protest any discrepancies.

PLAYING THE MARKETS

CONTENTS

Chapter 14: How the Stock Market Works
78

Chapter 15: Bonds: More Than Just Interest Rates
88

Chapter 16: Cash Investments: For Safety's Sake
94

Chapter 17: How Commodity Markets Work
98

Chapter 18: Mutual Funds: The Small Investors' Playground
102

Chapter 19: How to Make Sense of Stock Market Indexes
112

THE WORLD'S FINANCIAL marketplace is the best forum for exhibiting the complexity of money.

New technologies and money-management entrepreneurship have spawned a new era of global trading of securities. Securities are tradable investments that include "stocks" (ownership shares of companies), "bonds" (pieces of loans from businesses and governments), and "contracts" (rights to buy or sell raw materials, finished goods, and investments). Securities trade today from "Wall Street" (a catch phrase for American markets, dating to their roots on a street in New York City) to European *bourses* (French for markets) to the "emerging" markets in former communist-run countries and the developing economies of Asia, Africa, and South and Latin America.

The trading of investments has existed for centuries. Before the 20th century, trading often was a busy bazaar, with buyers and sellers informally meeting to exchange cash and investments. The American Stock Exchange was known as "The Curb" because traders stood in the streets of New York calling out trading orders to officials in windows of the exchange's headquarters building. In the early 20th century, more formalized marketplaces evolved. An American euphoria about stocks in the 1920s ended with the disastrous market crash of 1929. It bankrupted thousands and contributed to the economic depression that followed. As a result, strict regulation of securities markets was enacted in the United States.

The computer brought the next revolution. News about trades was once posted on chalkboards and transmitted nationwide on encoded "ticker tape machines" that printed information on narrow strands of paper. Computerization made trading data and other market news easy to process and disseminate, and allowed huge quantities and dollar volumes of securities to trade. New data processing allowed the birth of asset-backed bonds. These securities, most popular as mortgage-backed bonds, represent hundreds of loans combined by lenders who sell small slices to investors as income-producing investments. And thanks to computerization, average investors can get worldwide trading data on television, over the telephone, or on their home computer.

It would be easy to dismiss much of the broadened financial market's activities as a form of legalized gambling. Many professional investors admit that much trading and analysis is virtually worthless except to those people making money off the trades or the advice. Still, the daily trading of securities (with time zone changes, it's almost around-the-clock activity) serves numerous purposes.

The global securities markets offer incredible "liquidity"—instant access to invested money—to even small investors. This means that professional and small traders can quickly buy and sell stocks and bonds. Often, the confirmation of a completed trade takes just seconds, and cash from a sale is available almost instantly. Compare that to real estate deals that can take weeks to complete. Basically, it's easier for the typical American today to trade foreign company stocks than it is to buy or sell a house.

But liquidity is not always good. It creates a "trader's mentality," in which stock, bond, and commodity prices gyrate as traders jockey for the slightest edge coming from news or rumors. Instant access to money can also set off panics, since nervous investors can sell out quickly. Following the October 1987 stock market crash, U.S. regulators put a modest lid on liquidity. They established rules requiring U.S. markets to temporarily shut down to temper investor panic if huge price swings occur.

The constant market trading also allows investors to continually reexamine their strategies as economic and business conditions evolve. News that moves prices of securities such as new economic indicators, business deals, profit reports, and even foreign affairs developments occurs around the clock. So the extensive trading allows traders both big and small to review the merits of various markets or market segments for profit opportunities—stocks versus bonds; stocks of old manufacturers versus new technology companies; U.S. company stocks versus foreign company stocks; and more.

Financial markets play a major role as matchmaker. There are investors with idle cash looking to earn a handsome return. There are various businesses and governments willing to sell some slice of their activities or to borrow money to get needed funding. The most obvious matchmaking is the offering of new stocks and bonds. Sellers (businesses and governments) get cash from buyers (investors) at terms often dictated by the daily trading of old stocks and bonds of similar scope and structure.

The world's worth of new offerings raise tens of billions of dollars annually for everything from new plants for old manufacturers to money to keep young technology firms going to paying for the U.S. budget deficit to building needed infrastructure in developing countries. With the dramatic decline of communism's power in the late 1980s, once socialist governments now court investors to bring investment dollars to the epitome of capitalism, new financial markets in former communist countries.

The financial marketplace also allows for the trading of risks. Commodity markets allow a farmer to sell a contract to lock in a price for next fall's crop. The buyer might be a food processor looking to lock in costs, or a speculator willing to bet the farmer's price is too low. Stock markets let entrepreneurs sell off pieces of their business so new shareholders share the risks and profits. Bond markets let businesses and governments borrow huge sums of money without any one lender taking the entire risk.

How the Stock Market Works

STOCKS REPRESENT a slice of ownership (known as "shares") in a publicly owned company. There's one key reason people own stocks: The U.S. stock market from 1871 to 1994 produced profits averaging 9 percent a year, a better track record than just about any other investment.

But before you jump into stocks, remember that they are risky investments. While historically the stock market has proven to be a consistent money maker, there have been many sharp losing periods. In 1931, the U.S. stock market lost 43 percent of its value. In 1937, the loss was 35 percent. And on October 19, 1987, the one-day loss was 22 percent.

To avoid getting unnerved by the ups and downs, experts suggest using only money that you will not need for five years or more to buy stocks. That gives your investments time to ride out down periods. According to American Strategic Capital of Los Alamitos, California, from 1871 to 1994, the stock market lost money 30 percent of the time when looking at one-year periods, but only 11 percent of the time when considering five-year periods.

Also, experts suggest that you don't start buying individual stocks unless you have enough money to diversify your risks among a portfolio of ten or more issues. This gives you a chance to have some winners and some losers and still come out ahead. Instant diversification is one key reason mutual funds, which pool investors' money to buy stocks, have become so popular.

Stock picking is labor intensive. Don't rely on tips you hear at a party, hot stocks in the newspaper, or a can't-miss company recommended by a stranger. Renowned stock picker Peter Lynch advises people to concentrate on companies they know. The stock may be from a leading company in the industry you work in, or a favorite retailer that's always packed with shoppers, or a service company that does good work at affordable prices. But that's just the start. You must figure out whether the stock is worth buying.

While the price of a stock is its most obvious characteristic, price has little to do with the stock's desirability. To illustrate this point and other stock-picking details, consider the stock activity of two mythical companies: young, fast-growing Frantech Industries Company and old but dependable Pine Street Steel Corporation.

A stock priced at $1 a share has the same chance to rise (or fall) in value as Frantech's stock at $50 or Pine Street Steel at $10. But do pay attention to price trends. A sign of strength is a stock trading near its 52-week high. Weakness is a stock near its 52-week low.

Another key attribute of a stock is the "dividend," payments that are typically made quarterly. These payments represent the company's policy to give shareholders a piece of its profits. Dividend-paying companies are popular with conservative investors who like the steady stream of income. Historically, the stocks of dividend-paying companies are less volatile, too, than companies that don't pay a dividend. But a company paying a dividend isn't necessarily a better investment than one that doesn't pay. Many young companies like Frantech prefer to plow all profits back into the business.

Knowing the dividend amount isn't enough. By adding up the past year's dividends and dividing that sum by the stock price, you get a stock's yield. (So Pine Street Steel's 10¢-a-quarter dividend equals 40¢ a year, divided by $10, for a 4 percent yield.) Use this number to compare against other stocks' yields as well as other income-producing investments such as bank accounts or bonds. A higher-than-normal dividend yield, however, can signal trouble. It could mean that the dividend may be cut in the future, news that would surely cause the stock's price to drop.

Company financial data is very important to the stock selection process. Stock investors prefer growing companies because increasing sales and profits should convince investors to pay higher prices for the stock in the future. Unfortunately for investors, many fast-growing companies have gone sour because booming sales made the company almost unmanageable. So determining the quality of a company's management team by researching company documents is a must.

Profitability is measured in several ways. First, to put profits (often called "earnings") in a more digestible form, annual profits are divided by the number of shares of stock a company has issued. The result is called earnings per share. (In our example, Frantech earned $2 a share, $20 million divided by 10 million shares. Pine Street Steel earned $1 a share, $100 million divided by 100 million shares.)

To make profitability comparable, look at the "price-to-earnings ratio" (P/E ratio). It's created by dividing earnings-per-share into the stock price. (So Frantech's $50 shares are divided by $2 for a P/E ratio of 25; Pine Street Steel's $10 shares are divided by $1 for a P/E ratio of 10.) A higher P/E ratio shows that investors are willing to pay more for Frantech's profits than they are for Pine Street Steel's profits. That's not unusual for a fast-growing company compared to an aging industrial giant. Typically, you should compare P/E ratios against a company's competitors or against the entire stock market. (The market's historical P/E ratio is 15.) Stocks with high P/E ratios can be problematic. Often investors get too excited about a young company like Frantech. If Frantech were to fail to keep growing or stay profitable, the stock could fall dramatically.

Another key bit of company finance is "book value," what the company's assets (plant, equipment, inventory, cash, and so on) are worth. Book value is often expressed as a "per share" figure computed by dividing the total book value by the number of shares outstanding. (Frantech's $200 million book value divided by 10 million shares is $20 a share. Pine Street Steel's $800 million book value, divided by 100 million shares equals $8 a share.) When you compare the book value per share to the actual share price, you'll see if the stock market places a premium value on a company's business (Frantech's stock is at 2.5 times book value) or below it (Pine Street Steel is at 80 percent of book value).

These formulas can be applied to at least 8,000 major U.S. stocks. For simplicity's sake, let's divide those stocks into four groupings: growth, cyclical, value, and grandmother stocks.

"Growth" stocks are shares of highly successful companies whose sales and profits are booming. They could be large companies that are household names selling brandname products. Or they could be smaller companies with promising new technologies. Buying growth stocks is basically buying stocks at high prices and hoping to sell higher. These stocks typically have share prices near 52-week highs, above average P/E ratios, and share prices well above book value. Growth stocks can be good investments but come with many risks. Sometimes just one misstep by a growth company (such as big profits not becoming even bigger profits fast enough) creates a steep slide in share prices.

"Cyclical" stocks are shares in basic bread-and-butter manufacturing and materials industries—from cars to steel and from oil to metals. While these stocks aren't as risky as growth stocks, these companies and their stocks tend to ride the ups and down of the U.S. economy. The problem with cyclical stocks is figuring out the economy, predictions even economists can't frequently make correctly. Experts suggest buying cyclical stocks when they are low during an economic recession and waiting for an economic recovery and stock rebound to sell them.

"Value" stocks define the art of buying low and selling high. Value stocks are from companies in financial trouble or hit by economic downturns (including cyclical stocks) or those in industries currently disliked by investors for various reasons. Value stocks tend to have share prices near 52-week lows, have below average P/E ratios, and have share prices that are below the book value. While much less volatile than growth stocks, value stocks have risks, too. It can take years for depressed companies to improve their finances, and sometimes ailing companies only get worse. And even if the business improves, there's no guarantee that traders will bid up a value stock's share price.

Last we come to so-called "grandmother" stocks, investments for the truly skittish. These stocks tend to be from companies in highly regulated businesses, pay high dividend yields, and have relatively stable stock prices. Telephone companies and electric, gas, and water utilities fit the description for decades. However, such companies now face new business competition and may be branching into riskier ventures. In 1994, some utility stocks, for example, lost 30 percent of their value from their 1993 highs. It may be hard to find truly secure investments in the future.

But the success of even the best stock picking is subject to whims of the overall stock market. If stocks are in general disfavor, a "bearish" period marked by falling prices makes shares even in profitable, growing companies look bad. Certain economic conditions, such as rising interest rates (which make income-producing investments look attractive), are usually bad for most stocks. Conversely, if stocks are popular, a "bullish" period marked by rising prices (often occurring during the early stages of a national economic recovery) can make even poorly chosen shares profitable. Unfortunately, many experts say it is nearly impossible to know when to buy stocks during bullish periods and when to sell them during bearish ones. So that's why experts often suggest buying and holding well-researched stock picks as the most profitable way to proceed.

Stock Trades: How They Work

There are two ways that stocks trade in the United States. One is the high-tech Nasdaq (pronounced "NAS-dak," short for National Association of Securities Dealers Automated Quotation system), and the other is the venerable exchange system practiced most notably at the New York and American stock exchanges. Both systems link buyers and sellers of stocks. Let's imagine you want to buy 1,000 shares of two stocks, Frantech Industries, which trades on Nasdaq, and Pine Street Steel, which trades on the New York Stock Exchange.

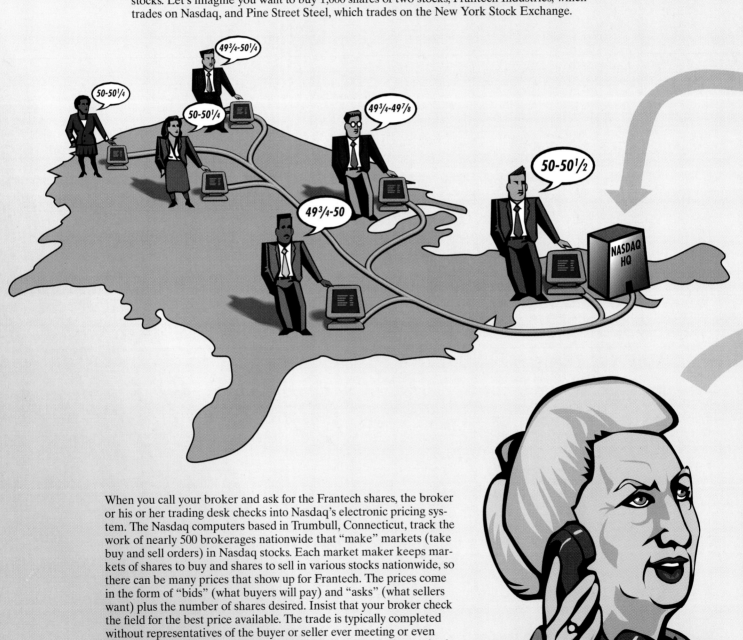

When you call your broker and ask for the Frantech shares, the broker or his or her trading desk checks into Nasdaq's electronic pricing system. The Nasdaq computers based in Trumbull, Connecticut, track the work of nearly 500 brokerages nationwide that "make" markets (take buy and sell orders) in Nasdaq stocks. Each market maker keeps markets of shares to buy and shares to sell in various stocks nationwide, so there can be many prices that show up for Frantech. The prices come in the form of "bids" (what buyers will pay) and "asks" (what sellers want) plus the number of shares desired. Insist that your broker check the field for the best price available. The trade is typically completed without representatives of the buyer or seller ever meeting or even talking. As you can see in the accompanying diagram, the best price is 49 3/4, or $49.75 a share.

When you call your broker for the Pine Street Steel shares, the broker (or his or her brokerage's trading desk) contacts their representative on the floor of the exchange. The "floor trader" goes to Pine Street Steel's specialist, an independent firm that is given the sole right to operate as an auction house for shares of several stocks listed on the exchange. At this specialist's station, either the floor trader can find another trader who wants to sell 1,000 shares of Pine Street Steel, or the floor trader will check with the specialist to see if there are any standing orders that could match your request. If there's no interest in selling, the specialist can either work the price higher to induce selling, or sell the floor trader shares of Pine Street they kept as inventory.

There are various ways to order a stock trade for any type of market. The simplest is a "market" order, where your broker accepts the best price available at the moment. If you want to set the purchase or sale price, you can use a "day" order (good for one day) or a "good-til-cancel" (transaction pending until your price is hit or you change your mind). A "stop loss" order is used when you own shares and want to make sure that you get out if the stock falls to a certain price.

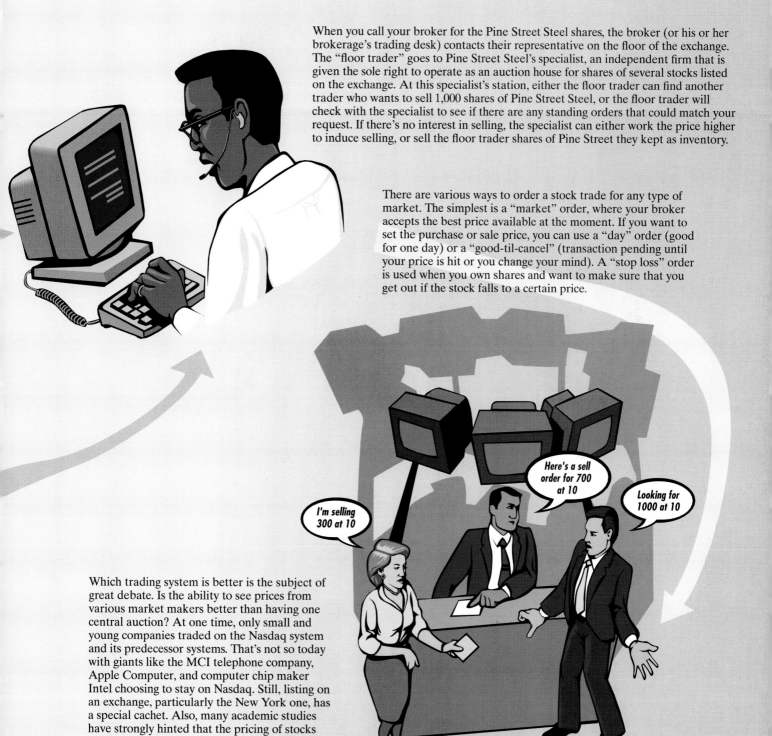

Which trading system is better is the subject of great debate. Is the ability to see prices from various market makers better than having one central auction? At one time, only small and young companies traded on the Nasdaq system and its predecessor systems. That's not so today with giants like the MCI telephone company, Apple Computer, and computer chip maker Intel choosing to stay on Nasdaq. Still, listing on an exchange, particularly the New York one, has a special cachet. Also, many academic studies have strongly hinted that the pricing of stocks on the exchanges is slightly more favorable to investors than that on Nasdaq.

Global Investing: What's the Fuss About?

Buying and selling shares of overseas companies has become very popular for American investors in the 1990s. For example, mutual funds that pool investors' money to buy foreign stocks in 1994 accounted for $1 of every $8 in all funds that own stocks. One reason investors like the fast-growing foreign stocks is because they broaden the choices available. In 1983, the value of all U.S. shares made up 54.2% of the world's major stock markets, according to Morgan Stanley Capital International of Switzerland. By 1993, the U.S. share of the world's major stock markets had fallen to 35.7%. Here's a look at how the world's major stock markets, worth $2.9 trillion in 1983 and $13.2 trillion in October 1994, are split.

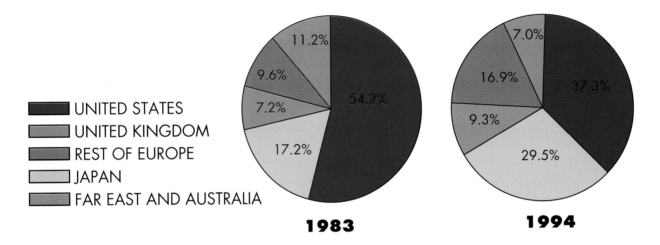

- UNITED STATES
- UNITED KINGDOM
- REST OF EUROPE
- JAPAN
- FAR EAST AND AUSTRALIA

1983

1994

Another reason that investors like overseas investing is that it provides an opportunity to get better returns on investments. The U.S. stock market rarely produces the most profits in any year when compared to the best performing markets around the globe. From 1983 to 1994, U.S. stocks produced average profits equal to turning $1,000 in 1983 into $3,978 in 1994. That ranked 14th for profits among the world's major markets. As a comparison, Hong Kong produced profits that turned $1,000 into $21,699. Here's a comparison of the profits the world's best stock markets and the U.S. stock market gave between 1983 and 1994, according to Morgan Stanley.

U.S.	Year	1st Place		2nd Place		3rd Place		4th Place	
29%	1983	Norway	82%	Denmark	69%	Australia	56%	Sweden	50%
6%	1984	Hong Kong	47%	Spain	42%	Japan	17%	Belgium	13%
33%	1985	Austria	177%	Germany	137%	Italy	134%	Switzerland	106%
17%	1986	Spain	123%	Italy	109%	Japan	100%	Belgium	81%
4%	1987	Japan	43%	Spain	38%	UK	35%	Canada	15%
16%	1988	Belgium	55%	Denmark	54%	Sweden	49%	Norway	43%
31%	1989	Austria	105%	Germany	47%	Norway	46%	Denmark	45%
-2%	1990	UK	10%	Hong Kong	9%	Austria	7%	Norway	1%
31%	1991	Hong Kong	50%	Australia	36%	US	31%	*Sing./Mal.	25%
7%	1992	Hong Kong	32%	Switzerland	18%	US	7%	*Sing./Mal.	6%
10%	1993	Hong Kong	116%	Malaysia	110%	Finland	83%	New Zealand	70%
3%	1994	Brazil	66%	Finland	52%	Peru	45%	Chile	45%

NOTE: * Singapore and Malaysia were combined for tracking purposes until 1993.

If you become a "global" investor, be prepared for even more stock market information. Thanks to varying time zones, stocks trade globally virtually around the clock. Here's a look at the trading hours (Eastern Standard Time) for the major stockexchanges in the countries with the 16 largest stock markets.

Trading periods for major market in that country

In some countries, there's a midday lunch break

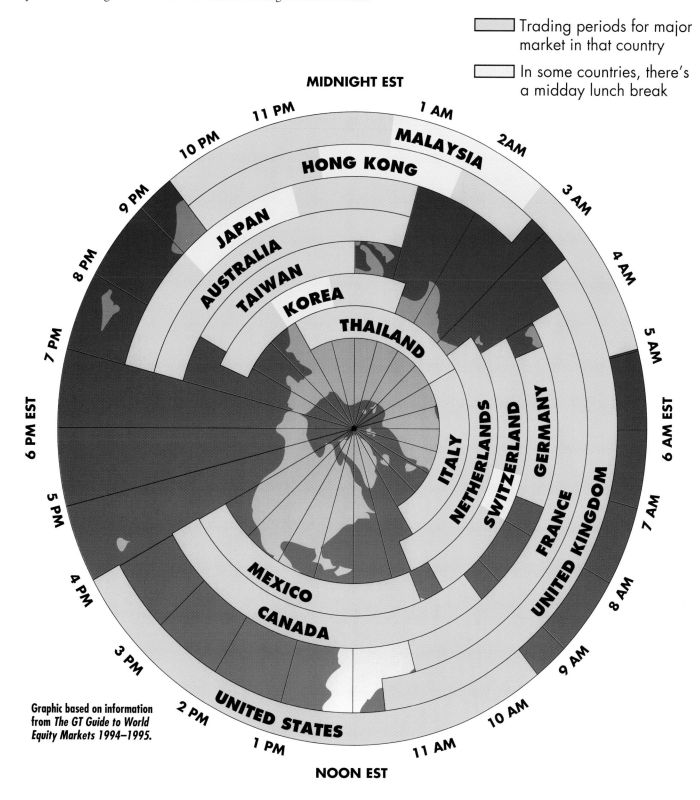

Graphic based on information from *The GT Guide to World Equity Markets 1994–1995.*

Bonds: More Than Just Interest Rates

ABOND IS A type of loan that is an interest-paying investment and financial obligation of governments or corporations. The bond market is the marketplace where investors shop for bonds. Bonds are favorites of conservative investors because they generate a steady stream of income from the issuer of the bond who promises to repay the full value of the bond at its maturity date. Let's take a look at five broad categories of bonds and some pros and cons of each class of investment.

U.S. government bonds allow investors to lend money to the U.S. government. Despite all of the nation's economic troubles, the vast wealth of America guarantees its bonds are among the safest investments in the world. The government sells bonds through the U.S. Treasury, hence the nickname "Treasuries." The range of government bonds that are sold includes bonds that mature in 90 days to bonds that take 30 years to pay off. The interest rates for key U.S. bonds are typically viewed as the best reading of where interest rates are headed.

Agency bonds or *mortgage bonds* allow various U.S. government agencies to serve as intermediaries between certain lenders and investors looking for high-quality bonds. These agencies buy loans—mostly mortgages, student loans, and farmland loans—then repackage them into large pools of debts. Then these agencies insure investors for repayment of those loans in full. This makes these pools highly desirable both for their safety as well as yields that are well above comparable Treasury bonds. Then, the pools are sliced into individual bonds—often called asset-backed bonds—and sold to investors. Through third-party "servicers," bond investors collect borrowers' interest payments plus all principal payments on their loans.

Corporate bonds allow corporations ranging from industrial giants to newer, smaller firms to use the bond market to borrow money. Investors like corporate bonds because they pay higher interest rates than government bonds. That's because investors take on "credit risk" when they buy corporate bonds. Unlike U.S. government bonds, there's a chance that the bonds' issuer won't be able to pay all the interest and the principal back in full.

Each corporation's credit risk is different, so several independent reviewing agencies give most bonds a "credit rating"—a confusing series of safety gradings that run from highest (safest) quality ("Triple A," with major reviewers) to so-called "junk" bonds (anything worse than "Triple B"). So

"AAA" is the highest rating (that's how all U.S. government bonds rate), not "A." But "A" is better than "BBB," the lowest grade that is considered a quality or "investment" grade. Below a "BBB" grade, bonds are known as junk bonds for their high-risk (but often high interest paying) position. Some bonds are sold unrated, a status that should raise the "red flag" of caution in your shopping evaluations.

Municipal bonds allow smaller government entities—from states to local institutions such as sewer or school districts—to also use the bond market to raise money. The biggest appeal of most municipal bonds is that their income is usually free from federal and state income taxes. This allows local governments to save money on their borrowing expenses because investors who lend governments money through bond purchases will accept lower interest rates. But just because municipal bonds are issued by municipal government entities, they are not viewed as being as safe as U.S. government bonds. Here, the same credit ratings apply as for corporations.

Foreign bonds provide an opportunity for even small investors to reach out and earn income from overseas governments or corporations. These, too, carry the credit risks of corporate or municipal bonds. (In fact, some foreign countries have defaulted on their bond obligations in the past.) Be very wary of someone pitching the often dramatically higher interest rates on foreign bonds. Why? There's an infrequently discussed risk called "currency risk." It translates to using your U.S. dollars to buy foreign bonds only to discover when it's time to sell that currency fluctuations—from the Japanese yen to the German mark to the Mexican peso—might return fewer U.S. dollars than you hoped for.

The bond market is often the ultimate referee on interest rates. With all apologies to the powerful Federal Reserve that tries to dictate interest rates, the bond market plays a role, too. That's because a world's worth of investors' opinions—evidenced by their actions in bond trades—can at times be more forceful than official pronouncements by the Fed.

And let's not forget that the bond market plays a big role as a banker, too. The bond market functions as the go-between for governments or corporations who need to borrow money and investors who need income backed by a bond's promise to repay all that was borrowed. All of these factors make the bond market a very powerful force.

A bond market analysis in the newspaper might read something like this: "Bond prices rose and interest rates fell today because fresh economic data from the government suggests that the nation's business climate is getting worse." While such downcast economic news could eventually cost you your job, they are a heavenly blessing to a bond investor. Why is this good news for bond traders? Because inflation frequently arises from nationwide economic strength. In these "good times," people and companies are willing to pay more for many goods and services. When inflation fears rise, investors sell bonds. That pushes down prices. And when there are few buyers of bonds, the sellers must push up interest rates on the bonds they own to lure buyers back to bonds. So the mass selling or the mass buying of bonds highlights the essential inverse relationship between bond prices and interest rates. Like an airplane with one wing tilted up and the other tilted down, bond prices and interest rates, too, must go in opposite ways.

Why should you care about any of this? Well, if you are an investor who holds a bond all the way to its maturity date, all this probably doesn't matter one bit. But most bond investors buy and sell their bonds at some point between the date of issue and the maturity date. To these bond investors, this interest-rate-to-price relationship is a major concern.

This relationship worked wonders in the late 1980s and early 1990s as a weakened economy pushed various interest rates to 20-year lows. As a result, investors bid up the price of older bonds that offered higher rates of interest from previous years. Owners of these old bonds not only made money from interest payments, but got a bonus: Their bonds were worth substantially more than they paid for them if they chose to sell.

Of course, when interest rates went back up starting in late 1993 as the U.S. economy finally began to pick up steam, the tables were turned. Investors sold bonds feverishly and bondholders experienced big losses on the money they had invested in bonds. Those losses easily outweighed increases in income that the higher interest rates brought.

PART 3

Shopping for a Bond: How It Works

Let's take a trip to see how a bond investor might go about shopping for a bond, also called a note or a debenture. We'll look at some of the decisions that have to be made and how an investment is found. Several factors have to be pondered when buying a bond. Getting the best price for a bond means that you'll be receiving the highest possible yield. It's a complicated chore, but one that's often worth the extra effort.

There is no central bond market as there is for stocks that have actual marketplaces such as the New York Stock Exchange to act as a clearinghouse. Rather, the bond market is an informal network of bond dealers. Some dealers and traders share the prices they will pay (the "bid") or want (the "ask") for various bonds through private computer networks. The actual trades are frequently conducted over the telephone.

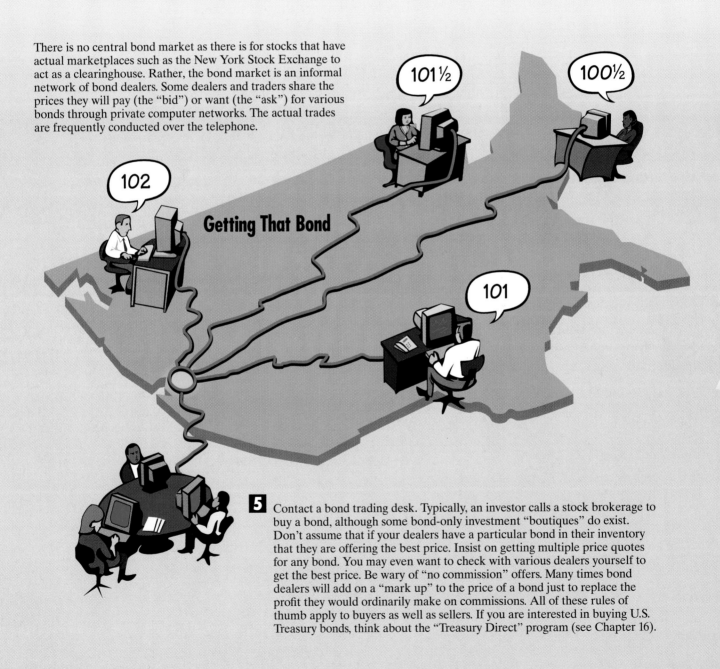

Getting That Bond

5 Contact a bond trading desk. Typically, an investor calls a stock brokerage to buy a bond, although some bond-only investment "boutiques" do exist. Don't assume that if your dealers have a particular bond in their inventory that they are offering the best price. Insist on getting multiple price quotes for any bond. You may even want to check with various dealers yourself to get the best price. Be wary of "no commission" offers. Many times bond dealers will add on a "mark up" to the price of a bond just to replace the profit they would ordinarily make on commissions. All of these rules of thumb apply to buyers as well as sellers. If you are interested in buying U.S. Treasury bonds, think about the "Treasury Direct" program (see Chapter 16).

1 Who's standing behind this bond? The best way to estimate a bond's safety is to check up on the issuing company's credit rating from reviews done by independent analysts. Ratings by major reviewers, such as Standard & Poor's Corporation or Moody's Investors Service, are scored somewhat like school grades. The review score runs from A to D with a twist, multiple letters are better than a single-letter rating within each letter category.

2 What's the interest rate? The stated or "coupon" rate of the bond is what the issuing company pays based on the bond's face value, or how much will be paid back at maturity. But the coupon rate rarely reflects the interest rate investors might get if they bought an older bond from traders in the bond market. Prices of old bonds typically vary from that face or "par" value. Ask for the "yield to maturity" from a broker to get a figure that makes comparisons easy. (Do-it-yourselfers can follow these four steps: Subtract the market price from the face value; divide the result by the number of years before the bond matures; add to that result the amount of annual interest payments the bond generates; then divide that result by the midpoint between the face value and the market price. Got it?)

3 What's the maturity? In a historical context, the longer the maturity the higher the yield. So why not just buy long-term bonds? Because longer-term bond prices are highly sensitive to interest rate swings. According to Vanguard Funds of Valley Forge, Pennsylvania, a 20-year bond yielding 8 percent would lose *17 percent* of its price value if interest rates rose 2 full percentage points. As a comparison, a 2½-year bond would lose *4 percent* of its value if rates rose 2 percentage points. Furthermore, locking in to a high-yield, long-term, fixed return can become a money-losing proposition if inflation increases significantly. (Conversely, high-rate old bonds become more desirable when rates fall.) So, being a yield hog is not always your wisest bet.

4 Check the fine print. Small details can make a world of difference in the bond market. Some subtleties include callability, convertibility, and subordination. *Callability* is the issuer's ability to "call" the bond, or pay off the principal owed at an earlier date. This often occurs when interest rates are falling and a company or government wants to refinance old, expensive dates at a lower rate. *Convertibility* offers the owner the right to trade in the bond and receive stock in the company at a predetermined conversion rate. These "convertible" bonds offer investors the safety of a bond while also offering a chance to profit when a company's stock price rises. *Subordination* allows companies to rank the repayment of bonds; not all bonds are created equal if the company gets into trouble. "Senior" bonds stand the best chance to be repaid. Owners of "junior" or "subordinated" bonds will fall further back in the line for repayment if troubles arise.

CHAPTER 16

Cash Investments: For Safety's Sake

CASH INVESTMENTS, a collection of low-risk places to store idle money, are no way to make a killing. Rather they're a way to eke out modest returns while waiting for something good (a buying opportunity) or something bad (market turbulence) to happen.

Although there is no list of official cash investments, any asset that would qualify must be an interest-bearing note from a high-quality issuer; be short term, or be highly liquid, that is, ready for use at a moment's notice; and must carry virtual guarantees of the return of principal. Basically, cash investors make money by lending a bank, company, or government their money.

So when an investor says they're in "cash," their money will be invested in secure places such as treasury bills, certificates of deposit, commercial paper, and money market funds.

Treasury bills are short-term debts of the U.S. government that are considered among the safest investments because of Uncle Sam's guarantee. T-bill's interest rates move up or down along with changes in the markets that determine interest rates every day.

Certificates of deposit (CDs) are bankers' popular savings products that have federal deposit insurance against the loss of principal up to $100,000. Unlike T-bills, CD interest rates can lag behind movements in broader credit markets. Their liquidity is sometimes limited because of penalties imposed if the deposited money is withdrawn before the certificate matures.

Commercial paper investments are actually pieces of short-term loans of major corporations with top-shelf ratings for safety and financial soundness. Typically, they pay yields above similar T-bills because they are uninsured. They are hard for small investors to obtain, though.

Money market mutual funds are low-risk pools of investors' money handled by money managers who buy a mix of the previously described cash investments. Although no insurance backs money funds, the fund industry has maintained the strong safety reputation of these investments.

Cash investments are not just for the highly risk-averse. Professional money managers use them as hedges against falling prices in stock or bond markets. Corporate treasurers use them as a place to park surplus funds. And, financial experts tell small investors to keep an emergency fund in cash equal to three to six months of a household's income.

According to economic principles, cash investments should pay little more than the inflation rate. Figures from American Strategic Capital of Los Alamitos, California, show that in 1944–1994, the average T-bill beat inflation by only 0.25 percent.

How Uncle Sam's Treasury Bill Auction Works

TREASURY BILLS

3 MONTH
6 MONTH
1 YEAR

1 Treasury bills are popular with investors because they are considered safe. They are sold almost every week by the U.S. government. To start a sale, the U.S. Treasury announces the terms of an offering, which consist of the maturity of the bills to be sold and how much, in dollars, will be sold.

2 The Federal Reserve (the Fed) then accepts tenders, or bids for the T-bills, on the auction day. Bidders can be divided into three key groups: primary government bond dealers; independent investors and other brokerages; and the general public, making so-called "noncompetitive" bids that win the average bid's rate.

The Bidders

Primary dealers   These are the major Wall Street brokerages and large banks who are official U.S. Treasury securities go-betweens. As part of that role, they must submit bids at every auction. They also bid on behalf of their clients.

Wealthy types   Large investors, money managers, and other brokerages also can make bids at the auction.

Small investors   Through the government's "Treasury Direct" program, the average citizen can also participate. For a minimum of $10,000, they can receive a "noncompetitive" bid that guarantees them T-bills with an interest rate equal to the average rate on a winning bid.

3 Once the bidding closes, the Fed then ranks each bid by its dollar amount and the interest rate requested for it. As an example, consider this scenario:

> An auction for $11 billion in 6-month T-bills got
> $5 billion in bids at 6.00%; $2 billion in bids at 6.01%;
> $6 billion in bids at 6.02%;
> and $1 billion in noncompetitive bids.

4 In the competitive bidding system, all noncompetitive bids are automatically accepted. Then, the lowest yielding bids win.

> In our example,
> $1 billion in T-bills went to noncompetitive bids;
> all the bids ($7 billion) at 6.00% and 6.01% were accepted.
> That left $3 billion for those who bid 6.02%; half of the $6 billion bid were accepted.
>
> Noncompetitive bids earn the average yield, in this case, 6.008%

5 T-bills are then sold at what investors call a "discount price." So a $10,000 bill at 6.008% would cost $9,710 and would pay back $10,000 in six months.

How does Treasury Direct work?

(1) Get an application from your local Federal Reserve Bank office.

(2) Select an auction you are interested in. Most Mondays, three-month and six-month bills are auctioned; once a month, one-year bills are sold.

(3) You must send a completed application and a check for at least $10,000 to the Federal Reserve. It must reach the Fed by 9 a.m. on the day of the auction you requested.

How Commodity Markets Work

"COMMODITY MARKETS" ARE where investors trade risks in the future prices of goods (such as corn, wheat, crude oil, beef, or gold) or the direction of financial items (such as interest rates, the U.S. stock market, or the Japanese yen). While gold is a frequently discussed commodity price, U.S. interest rates are the most popular when it comes to trading activity. Playing these markets is a high stakes game where profits and losses can be huge.

Specifically, investors in commodity markets trade contracts to buy or sell particular goods or financial items at preestablished quantities, price, and delivery date. Interestingly, it is possible to sell a contract before you buy it. Someone who sells a contract first is typically betting that the commodity's price will fall.

There are two types of commodity contracts, "futures" and "options." Both create "leverage," which means a tiny price change in the commodity creates big profits or losses on the contracts that control large quantities of that commodity. A futures contract is an agreement to buy or sell a commodity at a set price in the future. Futures are so chancy that you can lose more than you invested if you bet wrong. An options contract is only an option—not an obligation—to buy or sell a futures contract for a commodity. This type of contract limits your losses on options to the original investment, if you bet incorrectly.

Various people use commodity markets to "hedge" the damage of price swings. For example, a farmer who needs certain prices for crops may sell those crops in advance of harvest as futures. The buyer of those futures could be a food company protecting itself from rising prices.

But hedging risks is only part of the commodity game. "Speculators," investors who bet on price swings, eliminate the need for a perfect match of buyers and sellers of a risk. So a speculator, rather than a food company, might buy a farmer's contract to sell the crop-price risk. The speculator bets that the farmer's price is lower than what the speculator can get later.

Commodity trading drew the national spotlight in 1994 when it was revealed that President Clinton's wife, Hillary, turned a $1,000 investment into $99,000 by successfully speculating on the movement in cattle prices in 1978 and 1979. While being a speculator is not an easy way to make money, Mrs. Clinton certainly beat the odds. Experts estimate that 80 percent of commodity speculators lose money.

Commodity Trading: The Method Behind the Madness

A commodity market's trading pit is one of the wildest spectacles in the financial world. Traders go face to face with each other, shouting or hand signaling buy and sell orders in what is called the "open outcry" auction system of trading. Here's a look at how an investor's trading request is completed.

1 Customer calls his or her brokerage and requests a trade to be made.

2 The brokerage relays the trade information to their trading desk at the proper commodity exchange. Various exchanges around the country specialize in certain commodity contracts.

3 At the exchange's trading floor, the brokerage's trading desk gets the trade request by telephone or from a computerized system. The order is readied for the trading floor and time stamped.

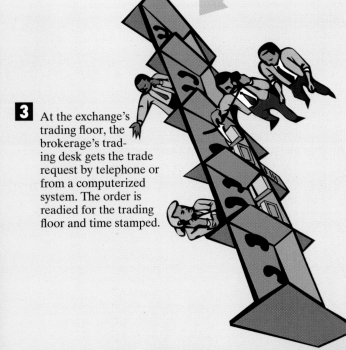

4 An exchange clerk known as a "runner" gets the trade order and goes to the pit specified for the requested commodity. In the pit are "traders," who work only for themselves, and "brokers," who handle customer orders. The pit is divided into smaller groups trading specific contracts for that commodity. The runner signals a broker to make the requested trade.

5 Each broker or trader acts as his or her own auctioneer. Depending on the level of activity at the time, the broker requests the trade either by shouting the order or by using hand signals. A trader or broker will respond in kind, making the trade good. The broker notes on the trade order the time, price, and quantity of the trade.

6 The order information is then relayed to an exchange official standing near the pit. The information is next sent to the exchange's price monitors. The exchange's computers in turn disseminate the trade to market watchers worldwide.

Here's a look at some hand signals used by traders:

zero   one   two   three   four   five

six   seven   eight

nine   ten

7 A runner then returns the order to the trading desk of the customer's brokerage.

8 The customer is then notified of the details of his or her trade.

CHAPTER
18

Mutual Funds: The Small Investors' Playground

"MUTUAL FUNDS" ARE professionally managed pools of investors' money that are invested according to predetermined investment strategies. They have gained widespread acceptance as an easy way for a small investor to play the financial markets.

Funds offer investors the chance to cheaply own hundreds of investments, from stocks to bonds to bank account substitutes. They are simple to buy and sell, and give investors good access to their money. They also instantly provide investors a diversified portfolio of investments, a tactic that cuts an investor's risk of picking just a few winning stocks or bonds. With their buying power and trading savvy, funds offer small investors access to markets previously reserved for only the wealthy. Although funds are a relatively reliable way to invest, the dizzying growth of the industry has resulted in a huge menu of funds to choose from. This is why investors must do their homework before picking a fund. (For simplicity's sake, this chapter is limited to "open-end" funds that constantly sell new shares. "Closed-end" funds, which sell shares once, are just a fraction of the fund universe.)

Fund companies gather money to invest either directly from the public or through investment brokers and planners. The fund industry is loosely divided along those lines. "No-load" or "low-load" funds cater to do-it-yourself investors who buy investments directly from the fund company and pay low or no sales fees. "Load" funds are typically peddled by investment counselors who get paid a sales fee or commission that runs as high as $6 for each $100 invested. All fund investors, whether they paid a sales fee or not, are charged various management fees by the fund company. These charges vary wildly but average $1 a year for every $100 held by the fund.

The current form of mutual funds evolved from the Investment Company Act of 1940, a U.S. law that was designed to clean up the reputation of investment pools tarnished by numerous debacles during the 1930s. Funds languished in relative obscurity until the late 1970s, when the industry's money market mutual funds, or "money funds," became a hit. In those days, interest rates soared to record heights, but federal laws limited how much a banker could pay savers, especially on smaller accounts. So money funds pooled investors' money and bought high-yielding, big-dollar bank accounts and short-term obligations of governments and corporations, investments typically owned only by the rich. Since money fund yields easily beat those of bank accounts, billions of dollars poured in. It was the start of a fund revolution helped in part by an unprecedented string of profitable years for stock and bond markets in the 1980s. The fund industry, which controlled less than $50 billion in assets in 1975, grew to $1 trillion by 1990 and passed the $2 trillion mark in 1993.

Before the money funds' ascent, those who used funds invariably chose stock funds. These funds give investors easy access to a diversified portfolio of stocks chosen through various strategies. Some stock fund managers can choose from the world's worth of investment opportunities. Other stock funds are limited to narrow slices of the stock market, such as a certain investment selection style, stocks in a certain industry, or stocks of companies with similar "market capitalization" (the combined value of all shares).

"Growth" funds are the most prominent stock funds. These funds tend to own shares of fast-growing companies selected using varying methodologies. The typical goal of these funds is to outperform the broad stock market, usually measured by changes in the Standard & Poor's 500 index. Some managers concentrate on shares of bigger, more-established companies often called "blue chips." Others choose from stocks of smaller, lesser-known companies. Some growth funds rely on "quantitative" analysis of stocks—computer programs that review company financial records and do much of the stock selection based on the manager's investment criteria. "Value" funds specialize in finding stocks of companies in distress or disliked by investors that are likely to rebound.

While growth funds tend to be volatile investments, "income-oriented" stock funds offer investors a steady stream of dividends and more stable share prices. These funds own stocks of dividend-paying companies and stock-like investments such as convertible bonds (bonds that can be swapped for a company's stock) and preferred shares (high dividend paying stock) to produce income for shareholders. Some income funds specialize in such areas as utility company shares or real-estate investment trust shares.

Such narrowly defined investment goals are common in the fund industry today. "Specialty" funds allow investors to tailor their investments to include industries or other parts of the stock market they feel are most promising. Some of the better-known specialty funds concentrate on shares of companies in industries such as technology, medicine, and gold mining. Specialty funds tend to be extremely volatile investments and are best suited for aggressive investors.

The fund industry has given investors unparalleled access to the world's stock markets with overseas funds that specialize in shares of foreign companies. The lure is that foreign markets have historically produced bigger profits than the U.S. stock market. Investors should note that currency fluctuations, which alter the value of foreign investments, can make these funds doubly volatile. There are two broad types of these funds: "international" funds own primarily foreign shares, while "global" or "world" funds buy both U.S. and foreign shares. Many of the international funds concentrate on major foreign markets such as Japan, the United Kingdom, France, Germany, and Hong Kong. Other funds own shares in "emerging" markets of less economically developed countries such as Brazil, India, and the Czech Republic. Global investing has been a big theme in the 1990s. While in 1980 few investors used these funds, by 1995 roughly $1 of every $8 invested in stock funds was in some sort of overseas fund.

While stock funds get the glory from their handsome but erratic profits, bond funds actually draw as many dollars from investors. "Bond" funds, frequently pitched as conservative investments, own various types of interest-paying obligations of governments and corporations. In theory, bond funds are managed to produce relatively stable share prices and a steady flow of income. With stock funds, investors have placed most of their money in funds that own broad selections of company shares. With bond funds, however, funds with narrowly defined objectives get the most money. Despite their popularity, many experts think investors overuse these narrow bond funds. Funds with a broader mix of bonds should give investors better results in the long run.

Narrowly focused bond funds define themselves by the maturity dates of the bonds they own and/or the type of bond issuer they concentrate on—governments or corporations. Some funds even specialize in bonds from overseas. When it comes to maturities, short-term bond funds (owning bonds due in fewer than five years) tend to offer the least risk of loss in fund share prices while long-term bond funds (more than ten years) are volatile but should produce the highest dividends. Intermediate-term funds (five to ten years) fall in between. Government bond funds won't be hurt by bonds going into default, but corporate bond funds offer higher dividends. Government fund investors should be aware that although the funds own U.S.-backed bonds, fund share prices will fluctuate because of the daily pricing of bonds held by the fund. If you sell at the wrong time, you can lose money in a government bond fund.

Many investors like municipal funds that concentrate on interest-paying obligations of local and state governments and agencies. Interest from those bonds and the income that is passed along to fund shareholders is typically free of federal income tax.

Municipal funds are either national funds, which own bonds from across the nation, or "single-state" funds that own bonds from just one state and double the tax break. Investors usually pay no state income tax on municipal bonds from their home state. Like government funds, municipal funds also have share price risks, too.

When it comes to risks, few bond funds are chancier than high-yield or "junk bond" funds. These funds specialize in obligations of corporations without established track records or with finances in jeopardy. Since so much rides on the financial health of the company, junk bonds are much more like owning stocks than bonds. The funds' strategy is to own a wide assortment of these risky bonds so that a handful of problems will not overshadow the high dividends these bonds pay. Junk bond funds were fast sellers in the mid-1980s, but their reputation was blackened when junk bond prices collapsed in the late 1980s. Still, experts suggest that now that junk-bond prices have stabilized in the 1990s, a high-yield fund can be a good investment if viewed more like a conservative stock investment.

If you are totally confused about all of these alternatives, the fund industry itself will help you make the choice. Balanced funds own a specified mix of stocks and bonds, which in its classic form is 60 percent stocks and 40 percent bonds. Balanced funds have long been popular because this combination often smoothes out the bumpy ride a stock fund owner can suffer. Typically, balanced funds further cater to conservative investors by holding lower-risk stocks. A 1990s twist is the "asset allocation" fund. These funds juggle their mix between stocks, bonds, and risk-free cash investments. Asset allocation funds are tailored for the beginning investor who doesn't understand the markets or an investor who has little time to follow the markets. These funds attempt to catch the opportune moments to hold each type of investment. Whether they can sucessfully accomplish that trick for long periods will be interesting to watch.

How a Mutual Fund Works

Here's a look at how your money, and that of thousands of other investors, flows through the mutual fund system.

One key to understanding your mutual fund is the "Net Asset Value" (NAV) or the share price of an open-ended mutual fund. The NAV is calculated at the end of each business day by the fund company and represents the total value of all stocks, bonds, other investments, dividends, and idle cash of the fund minus all expenses (management, marketing, and legal fees), divided by the number of all shares of the fund. The NAV is the price you can sell the shares for. If your fund has a sales charge, you'll likely pay a higher "offering" price representing the NAV plus the sales fee. You'll find the NAV listed in most newspapers along with the change from the previous day. Some newspapers now include a longer-term performance figure, too. This number represents the "total return" of a fund, that is, the changes in NAV plus any dividends paid to shareholders. You can use these figures, based on time periods such as three or six months or one, three, and five years, to best compare how one fund is doing versus another.

1-yr Ret	Fund	NAV	Chg.
	Red Rock Funds		
+2.1%	Balanced	55.10	-.22
-1.1%	Bond	10.20	-.02
+9.1%	Overseas	4.44	-.02
+4.1%	Stock	27.75	+.44
	Remarkable Funds		
+0.1%	Allocator	22.22	+.32
			-.22

1 Investors put money in a fund either by direct contact with a fund or through an investment broker or planner. While the money is often sent to the fund, it actually goes to an independent trustee or custodian bank that oversees all fund financial activities. Subsequent trading orders are handled by the fund company, but your money actually stays in the hands of the trustee bank.

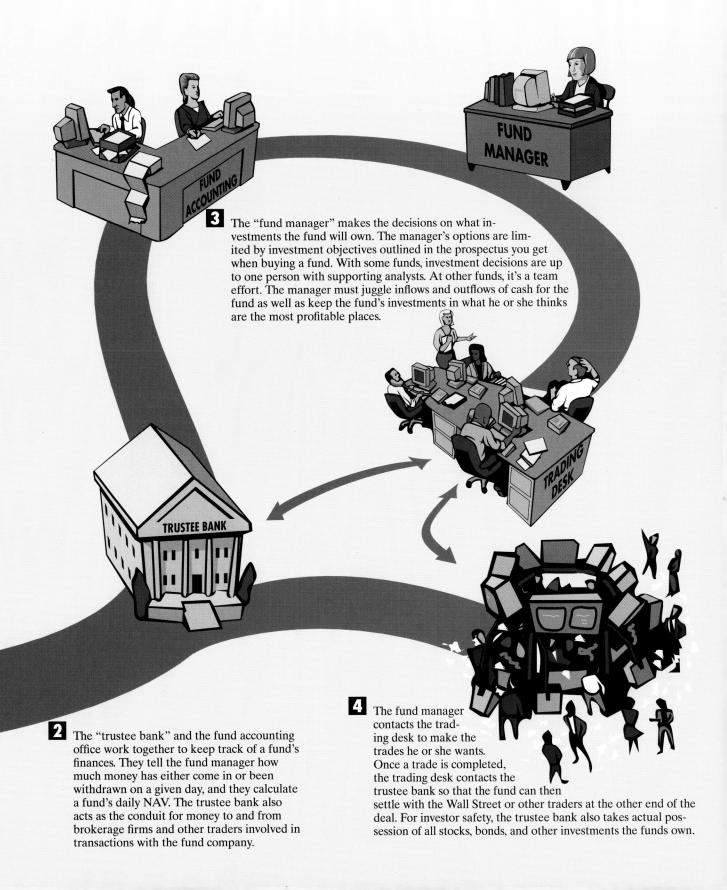

3 The "fund manager" makes the decisions on what investments the fund will own. The manager's options are limited by investment objectives outlined in the prospectus you get when buying a fund. With some funds, investment decisions are up to one person with supporting analysts. At other funds, it's a team effort. The manager must juggle inflows and outflows of cash for the fund as well as keep the fund's investments in what he or she thinks are the most profitable places.

2 The "trustee bank" and the fund accounting office work together to keep track of a fund's finances. They tell the fund manager how much money has either come in or been withdrawn on a given day, and they calculate a fund's daily NAV. The trustee bank also acts as the conduit for money to and from brokerage firms and other traders involved in transactions with the fund company.

4 The fund manager contacts the trading desk to make the trades he or she wants. Once a trade is completed, the trading desk contacts the trustee bank so that the fund can then settle with the Wall Street or other traders at the other end of the deal. For investor safety, the trustee bank also takes actual possession of all stocks, bonds, and other investments the funds own.

How to Choose a Mutual Fund

With more funds than the combined number of stocks of the New York and American stock exchanges, choosing a fund can be difficult. Experts suggest you match your risk tolerance to your time horizon (the time when you'll need the money you invest). Using the accompanying matrix, you'll find some funds that may fit your needs.

RISK TOLERANCE VS. TIME HORIZON	Under 2 years	2 to 5 years	5 years or more
SKITTISH: Fearful of losses	Money funds	Money funds Bond funds •Short-term	Money funds Bond funds •Short-term •Intermediate-term Stock funds •Income
INCOME ORIENTED: Willing to take modest risks to earn good stream of income.	Money funds	Money funds Bond funds •Short-term •Intermediate-term Stock funds •Income	Bond funds •Short-term •Intermediate-term Stock funds •Income Balanced funds Asset Allocation funds
GROWTH ORIENTED: Willing to take risks to grow investments	Money funds Bond funds •Short-term	Bond funds •Short-term •Intermediate-term Stock funds •Income Balanced funds Asset Allocation funds	Stock funds •Growth •International Bond funds •Intermediate-term •Long-term Asset Allocation funds
AGGRESSIVE: Willing to take large risks.	Money funds Bond funds •Short-term •Intermediate-term	Stock funds •Growth •International Bond funds •Intermediate-term •Long-term Asset Allocation funds	Stock funds •Growth •International •Specialty Bond funds •Intermediate-term •Long-term •Junk

■ CONSERVATIVE ■ MODERATELY AGGRESSIVE ■ AGGRESSIVE

Once you know what type of fund you want, you must choose what individual fund you'll use. You can do your own research by calling fund companies, going to your public library, and reviewing newspapers' business sections or financial magazines. Remember that there are numerous funds available, so you don't have to settle for something that makes you uncomfortable.

Risk

Can you live with fluctuations in the market that may affect a fund you've picked? Especially one with a handsome track record? Ask yourself if you can hold a certain fund through a market downturn. Ask for a stock fund's performance in 1987's fourth quarter and/or 1990's third quarter. For a bond fund, see how your choices did in 1987's second quarter and/or 1994's first quarter. Could you live with those losses? If not, find a more conservative choice.

Management

Check to see if the manager who established a fund's great track record is still there. Many funds today say that they're run by a "team" approach, however, so the departure of a star manager is minimized, at least publicly. Find out how other funds at the company are doing, even if you wouldn't buy them. Good companies have many fine funds.

History

A fund's track record is important. One key performance is "total return" (price changes plus dividends). The longer the successful history, the better. Shy away from the absolutely top-performing funds. Many top funds were either lucky or took big risks. Services such as Morningstar of Chicago and Value Line of New York provide analytical ratings—from 5 for best to none for worst—based on computer studies of fund records.

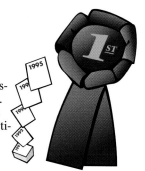

Fine Print

Read the materials that are given you when buying a fund. Unfortunately, many investors after losing money say, "I was never told about the risks." Often, the risks were printed in the sales literature. And many fund companies will provide additional brochures on buying funds and playing the markets if you ask.

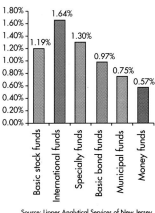

Expenses

If you're a true do-it-yourself investor, there's little reason to pay commissions or sales fees to buy or sell a fund. But over the long run, the expense to watch is management fees. These charges are quoted as an annual percentage representing the total costs of running a fund divided by the assets that the fund holds. Compare the management fees of similar funds. The one with the lower fee often has a better chance to make more profits.

MANAGEMENT FEES

Median 1994 annual management fees for selected types of funds.

Basic stock funds	1.19%
International funds	1.64%
Specialty funds	1.30%
Basic bond funds	0.97%
Municipal funds	0.75%
Money funds	0.57%

Source: Lipper Analytical Services of New Jersey

CHAPTER
19

How to Make Sense of Stock Market Indexes

STOCK MARKET "INDEXES" serve as barometers for the stock market's health. You can find stock indexes published daily in the business section of your local newspaper, hear them quoted on television and radio news reports, and find them on computer online information services.

Each index uses different companies' stock in its calculation, and indexes may be tabulated in various ways. The best-known stock index is the Dow Jones Industrial Average, comprising stocks of 30 large American companies. "The Dow," as investors call it, is synonymous with the ups and downs of the U.S. stock market. When people talk about how stocks are doing, they'll say: "The market's up 8 points today." What they mean is that the Dow is up 8 points.

But despite its popularity, few experts see the Dow as a good measure of the American market's activity. The Dow is disliked because its relatively small sample of stocks means that a sharp movement in one stock dramatically alters the index's direction.

Most professional money managers use the Standard & Poor's 500 stock index as their favorite way to view the U.S. stock market's progress. This index, known as the "S&P 500," comprises 500 major U.S. companies. With so many stocks included, no one stock really has any great individual pull on the index.

The differences between the Dow and the S&P 500 are not unusual. There are hundreds of indexes, each with its own characteristics. If you research a given day or year, you'll often find various indexes moving in contradictory directions. That's because different segments of stocks (for example, by dollar value of a company, or by industry) fall in and out of favor with investors at different times.

One basic way to use indexes is as a benchmark for your investments. Many investors set the goal of using their stocks to make more money in an up year (or lose less money in a down year) than the overall stock market. The goal for many investment professionals is to be more profitable than the S&P 500. If an investor prefers smaller companies' stocks, which are popular investments for mom-and-pop stockholders, they should look at the Nasdaq Composite Index. To track Japanese stocks, there's the Nikkei 225 stock index from Tokyo. Every country's stock market has one or more key stock indexes.

It gets even more specialized. If you own stock in a U.S. airline or a shipping company, compare its performance to the Dow Jones Transportation Average of 20 transportation-related stocks. Other indexes track groups such as utility stocks, banking stocks, and computer-company stocks.

Why Are There So Many Stock Market Indexes?

One key to learning about the stock market is understanding how stock market indexes work. It isn't unusual for indexes to give mixed signals because the stocks that make up the indexes may be acting differently. Here's a guide to some major indexes and a look at how four of them have performed in the five years ended September 1994, according to data from Bloomberg Business News.

Key U.S. Indexes

Dow Jones Industrial Average: Comprises 30 large-company stocks. Although it has many faults, it is most widely quoted index as benchmark for entire U.S. market.

Standard & Poor's 500 Index: Comprises 500 large-company stocks. Widely used as performance benchmark for professional traders and viewed as best guide to U.S. stocks.

New York Stock Exchange Composite Index: Comprises all shares on the NYSE, the nation's most influential. Seen as indicator of large-company stock performance.

Nasdaq Composite Index: Comprises about 5,000 stocks that do not trade on major exchange. Seen as good benchmark for smaller-company stocks.

Russell 2000 Index: Comprises 2,000 smaller-company stocks. Seen as best benchmark for those stocks.

Standard & Poor's Midcap 400 Index: Comprises 400 medium-sized–company stocks. Designed in 1991 to track stocks of companies that are neither huge nor small.

Value Line Composite Index: Comprises about 1,750 stocks. Seen as tracking stocks most individuals own.

Wilshire 5000 Index: Comprises 5,000 stocks. Viewed as index giving broadest view of how all U.S. stocks are doing.

AMEX Major Market Index: Comprises 20 industrial company stocks. An attempt by American Stock Exchange (AMEX) to produce its own narrow Dow Jones Industrial Average.

AMEX Institutional Index: Comprises 75 stocks heavily owned by large investors like pension plans or mutual funds. A check on how "smart money" is doing.

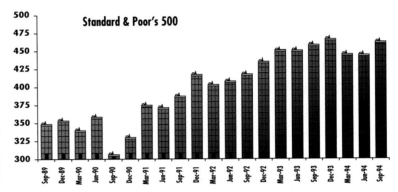

Big U.S. Stocks

Here's how the Standard & Poor's 500 stock index performed during the five years ended September 1994. The index gained just 32% in this period as the historic 1980s stock profits came to an end.

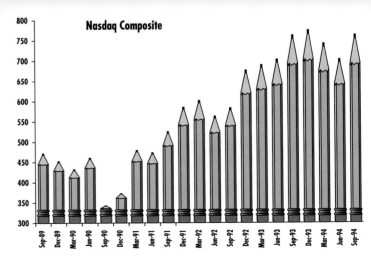

Small U.S. Stocks

Here's how the Nasdaq Composite Index performed during the five years ended September 1994. The index gained 62 points in this period as investors' favor for small stocks returned after a poor 1990.

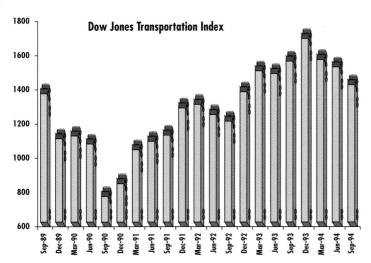

U.S. Transportation Stocks
Here's how the Dow Jones Transportation Average performed during the first years ended September 1994. The index gained a meager 3% in this period as fierce competition among airlines and shippers cut into industrywide profits.

U.S. Specialty Indexes

AMEX Computer Technology Index: Comprises 30 large computer and semiconductor company stocks. A benchmark for technology investments.
AMEX Oil Index: Comprises 15 large petroleum company stocks. Benchmark for energy investments.
Dow Jones Precious Metals Index: Comprises just four mining company stocks. Benchmark for such investments and indicator of expectations for gold prices.
Dow Jones Utilities Average: Comprises 15 large electric, gas, and water utility company stocks. Used to track such investments, popular with conservative investors.
Dow Jones Transportation Average: Comprises 20 airline and shipping company stocks. Good gauge for those who own such investments.
Lipper Growth Fund Index: Comprises 30 large growth stock mutual funds. This index can be used to track both fund performance and stocks of fast-growing companies, which these funds favor.
NYSE Financial Index: Comprises 400 financial, banking insurance, brokerage, and investment services companies. Useful as benchmark for financial stocks.

Japanese Stocks
Here's how the Nikkei 225 Index of 225 leading Japanese stocks performed during the five years ended September 1994. The index lost 45% in this period as Japan's economy, once the envy of the world, ran into trouble in the early 1990s.

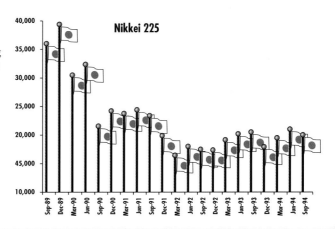

Foreign Indexes

Morgan Stanley EAFE Index: Europe-Asia-Far East index is compiled from 18 other indexes of stocks worldwide. Used as a performance gauge for stocks on world's major exchanges outside U.S.
Dow Jones World Index: Gives broad view of planet's investments as it includes some 2,200 stocks from around globe, including the U.S.
Japan's Nikkei 225: Comprises 225 large Japanese stocks. Most popular benchmark for world's second largest stock market.
Germany's Dax: Germany's "Dow," it comprises 30 major German company stocks trading on Frankfurt Exchange. One way to watch German market.
U.K.'s FT-SE 100: Called "Footsie," the Financial Times-Stock Exchange Index comprises 100 large British companies' stocks as popular gauge for that country's market.
France's CAC-40: Key gauge of stocks on Paris *bourse* from 40 large company stocks on Compagnie Nationale des Agents de Change (computerized trading system known as "CAC.")
Canada's TSE 300 Composite: Widely watched benchmark for Canadian stocks that comprises 300 major stocks on Toronto Stock Exchange, by far country's largest.

POCKETBOOK ISSUES

4

CONTENTS

Chapter 20: Home, Sweet Home
120

Chapter 21: Insurance: The Not-So-Comforting Choices
128

Chapter 22: Retirement: The Biggest Job
134

MANY AMERICANS WILL be asked to manage far more money and make much bigger financial decisions in their lifetimes than they ever imagined. They will do so in an expansive financial world with a range of choices that is almost unfathomable. So when deciding some of the more common large-dollar dilemmas facing a family, they will find numerous ways to buy insurance, borrow for a home purchase, or save for a comfortable retirement.

Probably no one adequately prepared you to dissect and decide the strategies needed to run a household's finances. And even if you have picked up a few tips, the financial world is changing too fast to rely on old information. Juggling big money—whether it be your home finances, your retirement nest egg, or your insurance needs—is a difficult chore in an era when borrowing or saving six-figure amounts has become almost commonplace for the average American.

Then there's the emotional part of making big-money choices, a factor that's often overlooked. It's one thing to comparison shop for a can of peas or a suit or an appliance. It's another to ponder decisions that if made poorly can dramatically hurt your quality of life. If big-dollar quandaries make you a bit queasy, you probably should think about investigating both the details of such big-ticket decisions and your own financial character. If you can't live comfortably with a financial decision, even if it appears to be the right one, it's likely it won't be correct for you over the long haul. One of the first things you must do to figure out your financial psyche is to understand your household's money management style as it relates to saving, spending, and borrowing.

Are you the type who likes to live close to the financial edge? Some people can be comfortable with only modest savings and a small financial margin of error if something unexpected comes up. Or are you the type who likes a comfortable financial cushion? Other people wince if there isn't a healthy balance in the savings account, even if all the bills are being easily met. Appreciating which type you are can help you figure out just how much money to commit in certain circumstances.

You also have to consider your feelings about debt. There are people who will do anything not to borrow money. It's not an unhealthy financial strategy, although at times it can limit your choices and opportunities. Conversely, many Americans think nothing of borrowing money, even at ridiculously high interest rates. While having no qualms about borrowing money at the proper times can be a financial plus, too many people don't know when to stop, and end up in financial trouble.

Another part of your financial character that can help you make money decisions is understanding how much discipline you have when it comes to money. Do you have a track record of successfully paying off debts or putting aside money to pay for a future purchase? Or is your household the type where any unspent money quickly disappears? Those without good financial discipline should concentrate on products that offer "forced" savings, where the money never gets to your wallet, or on products that tie up funds for long periods. Whole life policies or shorter-term mortgages, for example, may be pricey, but they get money moving into investments without much effort from an undisciplined saver. Families with more discipline, however, can consider lower-cost alternatives such as term insurance or longer-term mortgages that give more financial flexibility if you conscientiously invest the savings. One way to instill discipline is to take advantage of direct-deposit options, where money is taken from a paycheck or a checking account by an investment provider. The money is immediately stashed into savings. Employers' 401(k) retirement programs are a good example of this.

Risk tolerance is also another personal trait you should consider. Of course, most people say they are risk averse. But when it comes to money, being totally risk averse can be expensive. With insurance, for example, being totally insured is costly. Look at how much more an insurer will charge you for a policy with a lower deductible or co-pay—charges you incur before the insurance money kicks in. And there's a simple rule of investing that says the more risk you take, the more profits on your investments you should get back. As noted investor J. Kenfield Morley once said, "In investing, the return you want should depend on whether you want to eat well or sleep well."

So the question becomes: How much risk can I stand? As a starting point, trust your gut feelings. Many experts suggest that if your exposure to a risk is worrying you terribly, you should think about moderating your exposure to that risk. Also, get a better understanding of the risks you face. That may make you more comfortable with the financial hazards that confront you. Consider whether it is really worth spending hundreds of dollars a year on collision insurance to protect a car worth only a few thousand. Or consider the damage the hidden risk of inflation can do to your finances if you only own low-paying but highest-safety investments.

In today's information-laden world, it's often hard to keep your emotions from swaying your money management habits. Even the most hardened investment professional can get caught up in a popular wave to buy or sell some product or service. The challenge is to separate the facts from the hype while keeping your emotions in check.

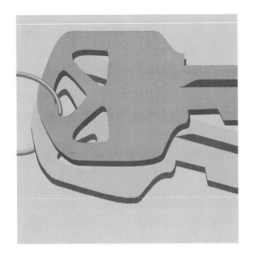

Home, Sweet Home

OWNING YOUR OWN home means that you are living the great American dream. With 64 percent of U.S. households owning their home in 1994, the country has one of the highest home ownership rates in the world.

Buying a home is certainly more than just a financial decision. Of course, you've got to have the money to pull it off. But you've also got to have the discipline and the desire to deal with the upkeep, the pleasures, and the headaches—plus the mortgage payments.

Home ownership expenses vary wildly among regions of the United States, no less within each locality. On a national scale, houses in the northeastern and western states tend to cost roughly 50 percent more to own than similar properties in midwestern and southern states. But overall, housing expenses have been falling in the 1990s, says Harvard University's Joint Center for Housing Studies. Thanks to falling home prices and lower interest rates, the center estimated that the national average cost of owning a typical home bought by a first-time buyer in 1993 was 30 percent lower than the 1982 peak, and just about equal to the costs in 1974.

Buying a home, whether it be your first fixer-upper or your retirement cottage, is no easy chore. For most people, buying a home is the single largest financial transaction they undertake. Expect a hefty amount of shopping before choosing one. You'll likely need an intermediary—from a lawyer to a broker—to help you cut a deal. Then there's getting a mortgage, as detailed a loan process as you'll go through. There's also the ream of paperwork required to close the deal. Then the real work begins—moving and getting your new household settled.

Before you decide on those homey choices—urban or suburban, ranch or two-story, three bedrooms or four—you'd better count your pennies. The major obstacle to most people getting their first home is saving enough money to make a down payment on the purchase. The rising cost of homes during the late 1970s and early 1980s made saving for the down payment an even tougher challenge. Numerous home buyers lost their chance to buy because they didn't have savings equal to 10 percent of the home sale price, the typical lowest down payment accepted by lenders.

But in the 1990s new loan programs offer opportunities for home shoppers whether they be first-time buyers or homeowners looking for another house. Private lenders began making loans requiring much smaller down payments. Some down payments are as small as 3 percent of the purchase price. Previously, such loans were restricted to a handful of government-supported plans for veterans, or the poor, or to buy modestly priced homes. You should note that these low down payment loans have some hitches. First, you'll have to have a nearly perfect credit history to get one of these loans. And you should be prepared to pay a much higher interest rate than the traditional "20 percent down" loan.

Undoubtedly, you will be told that a house is a good investment. There are many people who do make money owning a home, and many reasons why they do so. But just remember that there are no guarantees. For example, in Southern California, once considered one of the great places to own real estate, 43 percent of the sellers of homes in 1993 sold for less money than they originally paid for the home, according to Dataquick Information Systems of La Jolla, California.

In buying and owning a home there are lessons easily applied to other financial decisions you make. This is why many experts say that people often profit from home ownership. So step back and think about your home-buying process.

You'll remember that doing your homework is always important. Most home buyers do extensive research into everything from home quality to neighborhoods before making a decision. The same should be done for buying a stock, bond, or mutual fund. And in home ownership patience is a virtue, too. When people own a home, they tend to stay there (12 years according to a survey by Chicago Title). Virtually no one would sell their home because their neighbor's house sold for a low price. But often investors panic and sell stocks or bonds just because of a bad day or month in financial markets. And don't forget that every good financial manager needs discipline. Your mortgage provides a nifty automatic savings device. Part of your monthly payment goes toward building your equity in the home by reducing the loan balance. However, during the first five years of a mortgage, this equity is a small amount ($8 a month for each $10,000 borrowed on an 8 percent 30-year mortgage).

Even if you don't think of your home as a potential profit maker, you'll obviously enjoy the tax deductibility of the interest paid to your mortgage lender. Most property taxes, too, are deductible against income taxes. These tax breaks dramatically decrease the actual cost of owning a home. For a middle-income household, the federal tax savings alone is 28¢ for every $1 spent on interest or property taxes.

Two other tax breaks help those lucky enough to profit from home ownership. When you sell a residence at a profit, you do not have to pay any federal income taxes on the profit as long as you buy another home within two years that costs as much as the sales price of the one you previously sold. As a comparison, if you were to sell a stock at a profit, you'd have to pay federal income taxes on the gain even if you immediately used the sale proceeds to buy more stock. Homeowners with profits will find that Uncle Sam gets even more generous after they are age 55. After that age, homeowners selling homes at a profit can permanently shelter up to $125,000 of home-sale profits from income tax. It's an unparalleled investment tax break.

There is one tax downside to home ownership. If you happen to lose money on your residence, as did many in the late 1980s and early 1990s, Uncle Sam shows no mercy. The loss is no good for tax purposes. Compare that to owning a money-losing stock investment; such losses can be used to offset other income on your federal tax return.

Home ownership may seem like a dream. There are potential financial benefits, not to mention emotional windfalls to be gained. But it's not for everybody. First, make sure that you can really afford a home even if a banker will lend you enough money to buy one. Carefully judge the outlook for income in your household and think about any future major non-home expenses such as a new car or tuition. If you are really strapped for cash after a home purchase, the resulting feeling of being "house poor"—owning a home without having money to furnish or fix it—can be very frustrating. In addition, nothing can be worse than the constant pressure to meet a painfully large monthly mortgage payment if your household's income can't keep up with the bills. Losing a house to foreclosure is a very painful process.

Second, there's the argument that by renting a home rather than owning one you are basically throwing away your rent money. That's stretching the truth. Depending on where you live and your tastes, your rent may be larger or smaller than the cost of home ownership (mortgages, taxes, insurance, and upkeep). If it's cheaper to rent, you won't be tying up a large sum of money in a down payment, you'll have the flexibility to move quickly, and you won't have to worry about paying for maintenance. Plus, the money you're saving could be invested in other ways.

Finally, figure out how long you plan to live in a house you're thinking of buying. It's often tough to predict your economic future. But if you can't see living in a home for more than three years, you may want to hold off buying. Homes are costly to sell, with sales commissions and other transaction costs running as high as 10 percent of the sales price in some parts of the country. If you are forced to sell a recently purchased home quickly, without significant price appreciation in your neighborhood, you may end up losing money on the home after costs of the sale are included.

Keys to Getting a Mortgage

Making the right choice about your mortgage can be as important as negotiating the right deal for a home. Home loans come in various forms. It's important to know the differences before making a decision.

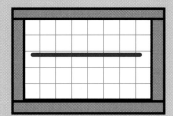 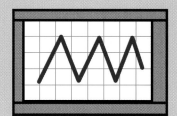 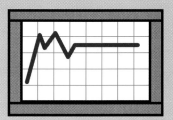

Fixed Rate Mortgages

This is the traditional way to finance a home. These loans offer the security of a stable monthly payment throughout the term of the loan. Since the lender takes all of the interest-rate risk of making these loans, you will find that fixed-rate mortgages can be the most expensive when it comes to costs such as loan fees associated with getting a mortgage. Fixed loans tend to be for 30 or 15 years. The 15-year loan can appear deceptively inexpensive. It does offer large savings on interest payments over the course of the loan. But borrowers should be aware that the tax benefits of 15-year loans quickly drop because monthly payments go largely to pay off the loan rather than to deductible interest costs.

Adjustable Mortgages

If you're willing to accept some interest-rate risk, these loans are cheap to obtain and often easier to qualify for. Don't shop just for the best discounted starting interest rate that ends quickly. Consider what financial index sets the loan's variable rates. Some indexes vary wildly and are best when rates are falling. More stable ones are best when rates are rising. The "margin" is the banker's profit above the loan's benchmark index. Margins vary at each lender. Also consider any caps that protect you from rising interest rates. "Caps" are either yearly limits on increases or a lifetime ceiling for the loan's interest rate no matter how high the index goes.

Hybrid Loans

These are a mixture of fixed and adjustable loans. Some hybrids have payments that vary in the first few years and then are fixed after a predetermined period. Other hybrids work the other way around. These loans are typically attractive to borrowers looking for low mortgage costs in the early years of a loan.

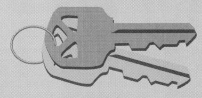

Here's a look at the annual average 30-year fixed-rate mortgages since 1978, according to Harvard University, and three adjustable-rate mortgage benchmark indexes in June of each year since 1978, according to Wells Fargo Bank of San Francisco.

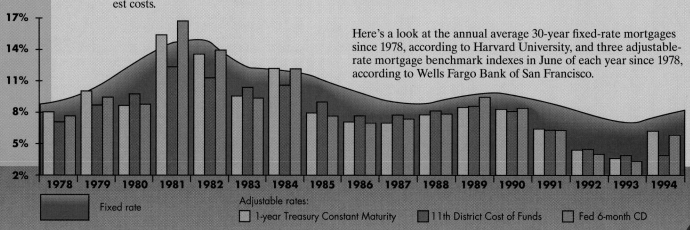

	Fixed rate	Adjustable rates:
		☐ 1-year Treasury Constant Maturity ▨ 11th District Cost of Funds ☐ Fed 6-month CD

How much house can you buy? Here's one way to look at it from information provided by Wells Fargo and Great Western Bank of Los Angeles, California. These formulas are rough estimates. You'll want to check with a lender afterward. Lenders will not only look at this type of mortgage-to-income ratio calculation, but they will also consider other debts you have as well as your credit history.

1 Jot down the monthly income of yourself and any co-borrower

$

2 Lenders typically will let you pay no more than 28% of income on the home. To determine the maximum monthly payment, multiply the income by 0.28.

×.28

3 Now you know how much a lender will let you spend a month on a mortgage.

=$

4 How much of a down payment can you afford? Lenders like to see 10% of the purchase price, but special loans go as low as 3%.

$

5 Now use the accompanying chart to find the largest loan you can afford with your maximum monthly payment.

+$

6 Now total down payment and maximum loan amount. This tells you roughly how much home you can afford.

=$

Maximum Loan Tabulator (for 30-year loans)
This chart tells you how much you can borrow based on various mortgage rates. Take your approximate maximum loan payment and cross reference it with interest rates you can currently get. (With adjustable mortgages, lenders often use the rate that will be charged after the initial discount is finished.) For example, a $1,000 maximum payment on a 9% loan equals a $106,000 mortgage.

Maximum Monthly Loan Payment	7%	8%	9%	10%	11%	12%
$600	$75,000	$69,000	$63,000	$59,000	$55,000	$51,000
$700	$87,500	$80,500	$74,000	$68,500	$64,000	$59,500
$800	$100,000	$92,000	$85,000	$78,000	$73,000	$68,000
$900	$112,500	$103,000	$95,500	$88,000	$82,000	$77,000
$1,000	$125,000	$114,000	$106,000	$98,000	$91,000	$86,000
$1,100	$137,500	$125,500	$116,500	$108,000	$100,500	$94,500
$1,200	$150,000	$137,000	$127,000	$118,000	$110,000	$103,000
$1,300	$162,500	$148,500	$137,500	$127,500	$119,000	$111,500
$1,400	$175,000	$160,000	$148,000	$137,000	$128,000	$120,000
$1,500	$187,500	$171,500	$158,500	$147,000	$137,000	$128,500
$1,600	$200,000	$183,000	$169,000	$157,000	$146,000	$137,000
$1,700	$212,500	$194,500	$179,500	$166,500	$155,000	$145,500
$1,800	$225,000	$206,000	$190,000	$176,000	$164,000	$154,000
$1,900	$237,500	$217,500	$200,500	$186,000	$173,500	$162,500
$2,000	$250,000	$229,000	$211,000	$196,000	$183,000	$171,000
$2,100	$262,500	$240,500	$221,500	$206,000	$192,000	$179,500
$2,200	$275,000	$252,000	$232,000	$216,000	$201,000	$188,000
$2,300	$287,500	$263,500	$243,000	$225,500	$210,000	$196,500
$2,400	$300,000	$275,000	$254,000	$235,000	$219,000	$205,000

How New Mortgage Money Is Made

Thanks to the help of government agencies, bankers are able to get money to make mortgages by selling the mortgages they make to investors looking for the income produced by borrowers' monthly mortgage payments. This "securitization" process enables homeowners and Wall Street investors to combine to make mortgage-backed bonds without ever meeting. Similar securitization strategies are used for education and farm loans.

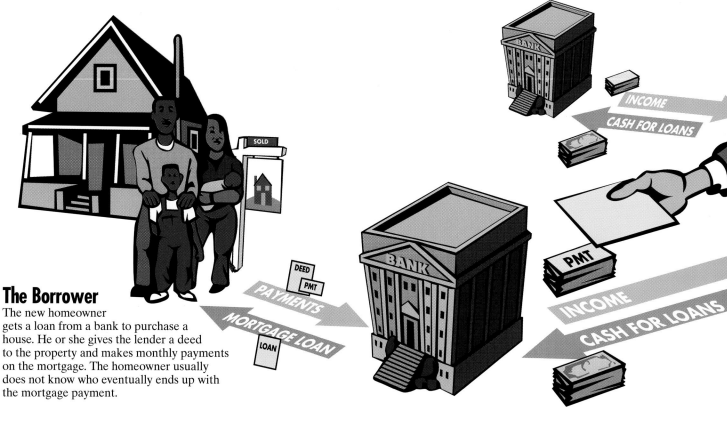

The Borrower
The new homeowner gets a loan from a bank to purchase a house. He or she gives the lender a deed to the property and makes monthly payments on the mortgage. The homeowner usually does not know who eventually ends up with the mortgage payment.

The Lender
The lender gives the home buyer the loan, which lenders view as two businesses: a stream of income from loan payments and the servicing of those payments. The lender often sells the loan's income stream to a government mortgage agency; this creates new money to make additional loans. Some lenders also sell the right to service the loan (that explains why the place you send your payments may change over the life of a loan). Servicers collect a small part of the monthly payment as pay for their work.

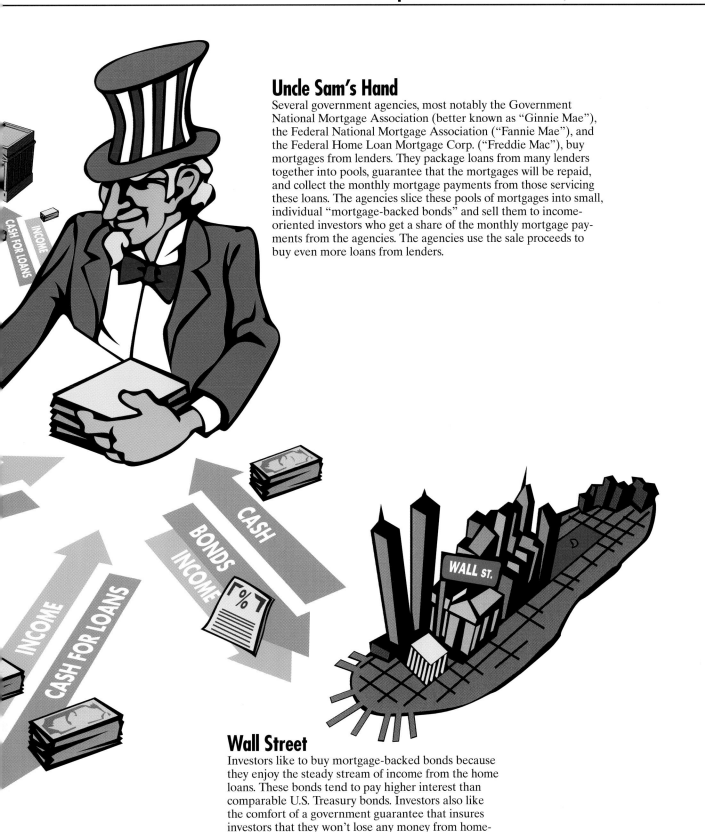

Uncle Sam's Hand

Several government agencies, most notably the Government National Mortgage Association (better known as "Ginnie Mae"), the Federal National Mortgage Association ("Fannie Mae"), and the Federal Home Loan Mortgage Corp. ("Freddie Mac"), buy mortgages from lenders. They package loans from many lenders together into pools, guarantee that the mortgages will be repaid, and collect the monthly mortgage payments from those servicing these loans. The agencies slice these pools of mortgages into small, individual "mortgage-backed bonds" and sell them to income-oriented investors who get a share of the monthly mortgage payments from the agencies. The agencies use the sale proceeds to buy even more loans from lenders.

Wall Street

Investors like to buy mortgage-backed bonds because they enjoy the steady stream of income from the home loans. These bonds tend to pay higher interest than comparable U.S. Treasury bonds. Investors also like the comfort of a government guarantee that insures investors that they won't lose any money from homeowners defaulting on mortgages in the pool.

CHAPTER

Insurance: The Not-So-Comforting Choices

NSURANCE IS BASICALLY a bet between you and the insurance company over when calamity may strike. You, or someone on your behalf, pay money (called a "premium") to obtain financial protection (whose details are set out in the "policy") against perils such as death, injury, sickness, or property damage.

If you knew if and when disaster would strike, insurance would be easy to buy. But since no one is given such an accurate crystal ball into the future, buying insurance can be a torturous experience. It can set up dizzying choices where a few dollars a month can bring tens of thousands of dollars in extra benefits, but only if disaster strikes.

You can buy these forms of financial protection from different types of insurers who vary by their ownership and the insurance they sell. Common types of ownership include private insurance companies, owned by stockholders; mutual insurers, owned by the policyholders themselves; self-insured plans, like those offered by employers who pay the claims directly; or government-run programs, such as Social Security or Medicare.

The pricing of insurance premiums is based on several variables. Most important is the insurer's estimate of the chance that you'll have a claim for a loss, such as an auto accident or a doctor visit. Almost as important as the frequency is the expected dollar amount of such a claim. These risks set the basic foundation to premium pricing. Another factor is your history of claims or your related track records, such as your driving record or whether you smoke. Insurers also consider the amount of the loss that is covered. So a "deductible" that requires you to pay a portion of the loss, or a maximum that puts a limit to your coverage, may lower premiums. And competition from other insurers plays a role, too. So always comparison shop.

Property and casualty insurers protect you from damage or loss of property and from any potential liability you might face from your actions or ownership of property. These insurers are best known for their coverage of cars and homes and for businesses.

Auto insurance is really a package of three coverages. There's the "collision" coverage that protects you against the costs of repairing your car after an accident. There's typically a deductible that discourages you from making a claim for minor damage. "Comprehensive" coverage protects the car when it's not being driven for losses such as theft, vandalism, or damage from falling tree limbs or a fire. "Liability" coverage protects you against losses you may incur from the car damaging others' property or injuring other people. Who is at fault is an issue in paying many auto accident claims. But several states have gone to "no-fault" systems, where your insurer pays your claim no matter what happened to create your loss.

Home insurance is also a package of coverage. A policy will cover you for damage that events such as fire or severe weather may inflict on the home. Flood and earthquake coverage typically cost extra. You are covered for damage or theft of the contents of your home. Home insurance also protects you from the liability that ownership of a home brings, such as an injury someone suffers at your residence. With both auto and home insurance, you should make sure that you have adequate coverage to protect not just your property, but also against the costs of replacing transportation and shelter while a damaged car or home is being repaired.

Life insurance companies' best-known product is protection against death and it basically comes in two forms: "term" or temporary insurance, and products known as "whole life" or cash value insurance. The products can be very complex. The key difference is that term insurance is pure insurance for the period you desire. It has no investment value and is typically the cheapest way to buy life insurance. Whole life products combine the protection of term insurance plus an investment portion. Money that goes into the "cash value" or investment part of your insurance policy can be invested in everything from a fixed interest rate payout from the insurer in a traditional account to pools of stocks, bonds, gold, or real estate. Profits made in a life insurance policy get the benefit of deferred income taxes and often policyholders can borrow against the cash value of the account. If you have the discipline to buy term and invest the savings, you'll likely do better because of the added costs insurance companies typically tack onto whole life investments.

Two other life insurance products are also worth noting: disability insurance and annuities. Disability insurance protects a worker against some of the loss of income due to injury or illness. For young families, particularly where the main financial provider is self-employed, this insurance may be more important than life insurance. That's because someone under 40 is far more likely to be disabled than to die.

Annuities were once thought of as an investment for retirees for a guaranteed monthly payment for the remainder of their lives. But the tax advantages of insurance policy investments have created great interest in annuities as long-term savings devices. Savers place money into annuities much like they would buy a mutual fund. Money from many investors is pooled to go into various investment objectives from stocks to bonds to global investments in a "variable" annuity account, or into interest-rate offers directly from the insurer in "fixed" annuity accounts. If you need this money back in less than 10 years, possible early withdrawal fees or tax penalties make annuities a poor choice.

There are few clear guidelines on how to choose a health-insurance provider, but references from friends or coworkers on the quality of care should figure heavily in your decision.

Health insurance has become highly confusing. It was not too long ago that many employers would cover virtually all medical expenses of a worker and the worker's family. An employee would visit a doctor of his or her choice, pay a bill, and get reimbursed by the employer or let the physician bill the insurance company directly. There was little or no cost to the employee. Today, most employers cover no more than 80 percent of a family's health bills. In addition, employees may have to pay for each dependent coverage, and a deductible will force an employee to pay for up to the first $1,000 of medical bills in a year.

Two cooperative-style medical groups are now also offered by employers as lower cost alternatives. The group coverages—health maintenance organizations (HMOs) and preferred provider organizations (PPOs)—limit your choice of physicians and clinics in return for low, per-visit fees known as "co-pay" that run $10 or less. HMOs are medical companies that run full-service health businesses from clinics and hospitals staffed by salaried doctors, nurses, and support employees. They sign up companies who then offer the coverage to employees and sell their service directly to individuals. Unless it's a dire emergency, someone covered by an HMO can only go to that HMO's facilities if they want the insurance to pay for the visit minus a co-pay.

PPOs are less formal groups established by either employers, unions, or entrepreneurs that sign up doctors and clinics who agree to provide discounted services for PPO members. Someone covered by a PPO would get to choose from any doctor or clinic belonging to their PPO network. The PPOs collect premiums from employees, and occasionally from individuals who sign up directly. The doctors and clinics in the PPO network are reimbursed for the discount they gave PPO members.

Retirees and senior citizens may also be covered by the federal government's Medicare program and/or similar plans at the state level. This coverage picks up portions of the costs of doctor visits, medication, and hospitalizations. Numerous supplemental plans can protect older people from any shortfall between the Medicare and state coverage they have and any higher medical bills. In many cases, seniors can trade their Medicare benefits for coverage by an HMO or a PPO.

Insurance: Shopping for Security Blankets

Buying insurance can be tricky because policies and prices are confusing. And your urge to save a few dollars here and there can whittle away your coverage, as well as the premium. Such savings may not be well spent. Here are some tips on how you can better shop for and use various types of insurance.

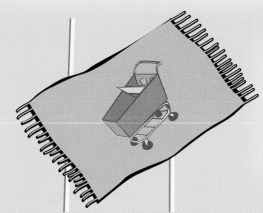

General Tips

Comparison shop. Policies for the same coverage can vary widely.

Be wary of unknown companies offering huge price discounts. Going with a well-known firm for a few more dollars may increase peace of mind.

If you have old policies, make sure your insurance is current. Have you had another child, added to your home, or bought a new car?

Store your policies in a safe place, and make sure a spouse or relative knows their contents and whereabouts.

Life Insurance

How much to buy? Five years of after-tax income is one rule of thumb. The average U.S. household with insurance in 1992 had $136,000 in coverage.

Buying lower-cost term insurance and investing the difference is a good bet for many people. Look at 10-year or 20-year term policies. They save money in the long run.

Try to use like policies when shopping. Yes, life insurance is very confusing.

Be wary of long-term projections of what an insurance company may pay you on investments.

Compare what interest rate you'll have to pay if you want to borrow against a policy's cash value.

Watch for huge start-up fees with an insurer's annuity investment accounts.

Young families, especially with self-employed workers, should think about disability insurance, too.

Most accidental death policies, including travel life insurance, are grotesquely overpriced.

One big plus of whole life is that profits in policies build up without income taxes.

If you have a large estate, whole life policies offer your heirs major tax savings.

Auto Insurance

Raising your deductibles may create considerable savings.

Consider dropping collision coverage on older cars to save money.

Check insurance rates before buying a car. You could save significant money with different models.

Ask about low-cost options that pay for the towing of a wrecked vehicle or get you a free rental car when repairs are being made.

If you have a clean driving record, look for insurers offering "good driver" discounts.

If you have good health insurance, see if you can waive the driver's medical insurance portion of your car insurance.

Home Insurance

Make sure your policy covers the replacement costs of your home, including any new building codes in your area if you own an older house, and your possessions.

Typically a low-cost mortgage payment option is worth it. It will make loan payments if damage makes your home unlivable.

Ask about discounts if you have auto and home insurance from the same carrier. Also ask about "umbrella" liability coverage in similar circumstances.

If you rent, make sure to get renter's insurance for your possessions.

Check any limits on coverage of expensive goods like jewelry or electronics. Buy additional "rider" policies if you need more coverage.

Keep a good inventory of your possessions. Videotape all your possessions. It will make any claim go more smoothly.

Note that home insurance typically covers theft of and damage to your goods away from home, too.

Medical Insurance

If you and your family are generally healthy, consider raising deductibles to lower costs. Lump medical expenses into one year, if possible, to get maximum coverage.

Health maintenance organizations (HMOs) can save you a lot of money, especially if you have young children who visit the doctor frequently.

Note what services are not covered and what coverage has strict dollar limits.

Keep good records of bills and payments. Don't be intimidated into paying bills that are incorrect.

Take up your employer's offers to set up flexible spending accounts, which lets you use pretax salary dollars to pay medical bills.

When switching jobs, you can be left without paid insurance. See if your new employer can offer you cheaper coverage for any uncovered period rather than pay for the often pricey mandated insurance your old boss will sell you.

Insurance Checkup

Price and terms aren't the only critical issues. To be a worthwhile expense, an insurance policy must pay when there's a claim. Despite what you may be told, insurance companies do go broke. Here are a few tips on how to check on your insurer.

Contact state regulators to see if the insurer is licensed to do business in your state.

See if your insurance commissioner tabulates complaints against insurers, so you can get a reading on the quality of service.

Inquire about the financial health of the insurer. Any competent insurance salesperson should be able to tell you a company's ratings with independent agencies. What's confusing is that an "A" grade at several agencies is the best review, while at others it's just "average" and "AAA" is best. Several companies track the industry. You're encouraged to contact them:

A.M. BEST: Covers the most companies. Its reviews of insurers can be found in many libraries. Best grade: A++. Write to them at A.M. Best Rd., Oldwick, NJ 08858, or call 900-420-0400 for ratings at a small fee.

DUFF & PHELPS: Covers broad range of companies. Best grade: AAA. Write to Duff at 55 East Monroe St., Chicago, IL 60603, or call 312-368-3157 for free ratings.

MOODY'S INVESTORS SERVICES: Well-known in investment world, it follows a modest number of companies. Best grade: AAA. Write to Moody's at 99 Church St., New York, NY 10007, or call 212-553-0300 for free reviews.

STANDARD & POOR'S INSURANCE RATINGS: Well-known in investment circles, it watches a wide range of companies. Best grade: AAA. Write to S&P at 25 Broadway, New York, NY 10004, or call 212-208-1527 for free ratings.

WEISS RESEARCH: Known for its scrupulous reviews of insurers. Best grade: A. Write to 2200 N. Florida Mango Rd., West Palm Beach, FL 33409, or call 800-289-9222 to get reviews for modest fees.

Retirement: The Biggest Job

SAVING ENOUGH MONEY for a comfortable retirement is easily the biggest financial hurdle most households will face and is the top financial concern of Americans.

Is the average person prepared for a job that involves investing and accounting acumen plus a good bit of economic guesswork? For some people, retirement planning means trying to replace half of their salary with savings in order to quit the work force. But national surveys repeatedly find that many American's don't have the knowledge, or the money, to retire comfortably.

Planning for retirement is a tricky calculation. If you are in your 30s, you have to make projections about your career future and what your life will be like in three decades. Meanwhile, you try to get the maximum profits out of your investments. If you are nearing retirement, you have to collect and tabulate dozens of figures to see if your retirement will work. At the same time, you must make decisions about pension benefits which are, in essence, grim bets on who will die first—you or your spouse. Once retired, you have to carefully watch your costs and manage a dwindling portfolio of investments that are a major source of your income.

But perhaps you are one of the lucky ones who get to retire in the last quarter of the 20th century. You'll enjoy a secure Social Security system paying handsome returns on the modest money you contributed. Pensions for corporate and government workers are paying generous benefits, often including fine medical care. And unprecedented booming investment markets in the 1980s and early 1990s fattened the savings today's retirees had socked away for their golden years.

For those planning to retire in the 21st century, things will be different. Previous generations needed little retirement planning. Social Security and traditional pension plans, the cornerstone of many retirees' cash flow, asked little of the worker, outside of paying Social Security taxes. Today, retirement planning is a hands-on experience requiring great discipline. And don't think of getting any lessons from previous generations. You're the first ones down this road.

There is great debate whether Social Security will survive in its current form through the 21st century. Changing demographics are putting a severe crimp in the system's projected cash flow. In the 1950s, there were 30 workers for every one beneficiary to help pay for the monthly checks. In the 1990s, that ratio fell to 3-to-1. And by 2015, it will be 2-to-1. Already, some Social Security retirement benefits have been pruned. Retiring at full benefits at age 65 ends in 2002, replaced by gradually pushing back that magic age to 67 for those born in 1960 or later. And there has been talk that cost-of-living adjustments for Social Security benefits, instituted in 1975 to protect retirees' income from rising prices, could be scaled back.

Then there's a somber outlook for corporate retiree benefits. Fewer companies—especially smaller companies, the nation's top job producers—are offering the traditional pension benefit. Some of the remaining older pension plans are in shaky financial shape. Between 1987 and 1993, the short fall of pension plans without enough money to pay future benefits rose by 163 percent to $71 billion, according to the government's Pension Benefit Guaranty Corporation. And while companies are legally bound to make pension payments, the same is not true for medical insurance coverage for retirees; benefits have been reduced by several major corporations.

All this turmoil puts the pressure on individuals to fund their own retirement. It's no easy chore. Most people assumed that their largest investment was their house. That's because someone else was building and paying for their retirement nest egg. A traditional pension generating $25,000 a year for 15 years is worth roughly $250,000 today. Without access to a pension, it's likely you have to amass a fortune of that size to pay for your retirement. Thirty years from now, to get the same buying power of the $250,000 pension, you'll need $1 million. Some Americans aren't taking the hint. A December 1993 survey by Fidelity Investments of Boston found that 34 percent of people older than 40 had less than $30,000 saved for retirement.

There are a few tricks to meeting your retirement needs. First, start as early as possible. It may seem ludicrous to be in your first job, and starting to think about retirement. However, you'll learn that time is the biggest ally of an investor. Take the scenario of twin brothers, Jon and Irwin. At age 25, Jon begins his retirement savings, putting away $2,000 a year for ten years. He then stops saving. Irwin doesn't start his retirement savings until age 35, when he begins putting away $2,000 a year for the next 30 years. If both brothers earn 7 percent, who has more money at age 65? It's Jon, whose early nest egg grew to $210,000 versus Irwin's $189,000.

The second trick is to use tax-deferred accounts such as individual retirement accounts (IRAs) and savings plans like the 401(k) programs to help boost your profits. By being allowed to defer tax payments on investment profits, your nest egg will grow even faster over long periods. And since you'd likely not need this retirement money for years, tying up cash in these accounts should be no problem. Consider a middle-income taxpayer earning 7 percent a year over 30 years. By using tax-deferred accounts, the resulting nest egg is boosted by 50 percent when compared with a scenario where taxes are paid on profits annually.

Despite some misconceptions, IRAs are still a good way to invest. Tax law changes in 1986 took away the deductibility of IRA contributions. So putting the maximum $2,000 in an IRA each year no longer lowers the tax bill for many Americans. With the tax deferral, IRAs are still a potent money-making option. For the self-employed, two specialized IRAs known as SEP-IRAs ("SEP" stands for simplified employee pension) and Keoghs (named after the lawmaker who wrote the legislation) offer greater deductibility and larger contributions. A big plus for all these IRAs is that the plan is all up to you. That means the investment choices are limitless.

The 401(k) programs and similar retirement savings plans at the workplace are even more powerful. These plans, along with 403(b) and 457 programs, allow contributions of $9,000 or more in 1995. Those contributions lower your immediate tax bill, and profits in the plan compound with tax-deferred status. Unlike the traditional pension, the 401(k) requires you to fund the bulk of the program, and you make the investment decisions. At many companies, the employer does make some monetary contributions to the plan so those who don't participate miss out on what amounts to a raise. One downside is that these plans offer a limited number of investments.

Another requirement to help meet retirement savings goals is to be aggressive in your investing. That means thinking about heavily concentrating on the volatile yet highly profitable stock market. Experts say that too many people are skittish with retirement money and put large sums in fixed-income investments. Over the long haul, stocks have consistently outperformed other investments. That message isn't getting through to everyone, though. A 1994 survey of Americans done for the Oppenheimer Funds of New York found that almost half of pre-retirees thought bonds were a better bet than stocks. The downside of being too conservative is that inflation will likely eat away at the buying power of your portfolio.

If you bet wrong, whether it be bad investments or just not saving enough, the result could be quite painful. You may have to work for additional years, or pick up a part-time job, to fund your retirement. Even slight investment errors add up over decades of investing. Say you earned only 6 percent, not 7 percent, while investing $5,000 a year over 30 years. The lower profits slice $77,000 off what could have been $472,000. It all adds up to quite a challenge.

How a Traditional Pension Plan Works

The traditional pension plan, also called a "defined benefit" plan, once helped pay for the retirement of many Americans. Not only were these plans free to workers, employees had little to do but get jobs and wait for the benefits after they retired. Today, these plans are becoming luxuries—estimates show that as many as half of American workers are no longer offered this type of pension.

You are entitled by law to a pension-plan description within 90 days after being hired, if the company offers a plan as a benefit. Terms include how many years one must work to get the minimum benefit (typically at least five), what the benefits are, and how additional years of work will boost the retirement payouts. Many plans call for retirement payments equal to roughly 1% of a worker's average salary for every year worked.

The employer is required to put away money every year to pay for all its workers' retirements. The employee puts in nothing. Pension experts, looking at variables like the age and salaries of the workers, determine how much must be put into the pension fund. (A company can waive paying what it owes only three times every 15 years.) Most employers hire outside professionals to manage the pension money. The employees have no say in how the money is managed.

Your employer must also give you a summary each year of the plan's activities and a benefit statement detailing what you can expect. Learn if your pension plan is "underfunded," where experts determine there isn't enough money to pay all benefits. Some companies do this as a cash management strategy, saying they are financially fit enough to pay benefits out of profits. For others, it's a sign of trouble. The government's Pension Benefit Guaranty Corp. protects retirees, but insures benefits only up to $29,250 a year; this organization is admittedly in financial trouble.

Once you're ready to retire, there are three common choices for how to take the money. Here's a look at the pros and cons associated with each option.

Single Life
This option pays the worker his or her monthly retirement benefits only for the rest of his or her life. While the payments are the highest, the risk is great for a spouse who could be left impoverished if the worker dies prematurely. Choose this option very carefully.

Survivor
This frequently chosen option allows a spouse to collect partial benefits if the worker dies prematurely. Monthly payments throughout the retirement are reduced. In return for further reduced payments, another choice guarantees the spouse monthly payments for his or her life, too.

Lump Sum
Some plans allow the retiree to get one large payment instead of monthly benefits. This is risky. First, are you up to the task of managing a huge sum of money? Second, check out the "discount rate" the pension is using to calculate your lump sum. Can you earn more?

401(k) and Similar Savings Plans: Why You Can't Say "No"

Few events have had a greater impact on people's finances than so-called "defined contribution" retirement savings programs for the workplace like the 401(k), 403(b), and 457 plans—all named for the section of law that created them. Rather than having employers pay and manage a worker's pension, these plans make the employee the major force behind the contribution for, and the management of, his or her retirement kitty.

There are three key elements to these plans, although the terms vary widely depending on the workplace.

1 Workers choose how much of their pay they want to contribute each pay period. Money goes to a third-party plan administrator chosen by the employer. Annual contributions for 401(k) plans, for example, can go as high as $9,200 in 1995. Contributions are taken out before taxes are calculated, so the plans help to lower workers' income tax bills.

2 Employers in some cases make contributions to the employee's account. This is typically done as a "match" to part of the employee's contributions as encouragement for participation in the plans. Basically, look at it as a pay raise. Many employers "vest" their matching contributions, so workers own only a growing portion of the match each of their first few years with the company. This is used as an incentive to get workers to stay at the job.

3 The employers, through the plan administrator, offer workers several investment alternatives. The decision is completely up to the worker. A 1994 law encourages employers to offer three or more choices.

Stocks
Workers get a chance to play the stock market either by putting retirement dollars into stock mutual funds or in shares of their employer's company. Experts say that stocks are a good choice for long-term retirement planning. However, don't own too much of your company's stock and leave yourself vulnerable if the company gets in financial trouble.

Bonds
Another common choice are bond mutual funds. These professionally managed pools of money buy debt obligations of governments and corporations and offer less volatile share prices than stock funds. Experts say that these investments are best suited in large quantities for people nearing retirement.

Cash
Experts think employees overuse this popular choice that offers low returns but investment stability. Cash may be money market mutual funds, a low-risk bond fund, or steady value accounts (or guaranteed investment contracts), a life insurance product that works like a certificate of deposit without the government guarantee.

Here's a look at some of the added benefits of these plans: 401(k) for general employers and 403(b) and 457 plans for workers at nonprofit and government agencies.

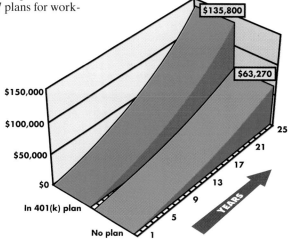

Tax Breaks: Contributions to these plans create powerful tax deferral. Contributions and investment profits are not taxed when they're made. Rather, taxes are due when withdrawals are made many years down the road. Imagine two workers, one who contributes $2,000 a year in a 401(k) plan, the other who takes $2,000 of salary each year and invests it in a taxable account. Both earn 7% a year. The first investor ends up with $135,800 after 25 years; the other, just $63,270. Even after paying all the taxes due, the first worker is ahead by roughly $27,000.

Portability: These plans let you move between jobs without losing this retirement benefit. If you leave a job where you have one of these savings plans, you will be able to either roll your savings into a similar plan at your new job or move it into an individual retirement account. Fight all temptation to spend these savings if you leave a job. Not only is there a large tax bill because of the powerful tax breaks involved, but there's a 10% tax penalty on top of that if you are younger than 59½.

Dollar Cost Averaging: Systematic investment encourages disciplined investing. By buying equal amounts of investments at regular intervals, investors are forced to buy fewer shares when prices are high and more shares when prices are low. Interestingly, this averaging tactic works best as prices are falling, and it lowers the risk of buying at the worst time. Look at how regular set-dollar purchases can work to an advantage in the example at the left. While at year's end, the share price was unchanged, its fluctuations during the year allowed dollar cost averaging to turn $2,400 into $2,833.

Dollar Cost Averaging at Work

Month	Purchase	Price	Shares
January	$200	$10	20
February	$200	$7	28.6
March	$200	$8	25
April	$200	$9	22.2
May	$200	$11	18.2
June	$200	$10	20
July	$200	$8	25
August	$200	$7	28.6
September	$200	$7	28.6
October	$200	$8	25
November	$200	$9	22.2
December	$200	$10	20
Totals	$2,400	283.3 shares @ $10 or $2,833	

How Social Security Works

The nation's Social Security system was started as a way to "give some measure of protection to the average citizen and to his family against the loss of a job and against poverty-ridden old age," said President Franklin Delano Roosevelt at the law's enactment in 1935. The system has grown in six decades to cover more people and offer more benefits. Social Security benefits go to retirees, the disabled, medical benefits for the elderly, and families and survivors of the benefit recipient.

Benefits are paid for by various payroll taxes, which have risen dramatically from 1% of income tax at the program's inception. As 1995 started, Social Security taxes (better known by the abbreviation on pay stubs of "FICA" for Federal Insurance Contributions Act) were:

Salary above $135,000, no tax.

Salary between $135,000 and $57,600: Employees and employers each pay 1.45% tax for Medicare elderly health coverage. Self-employed pay 2.9%.

Salary from $57,600 and below: Employees pay 7.65% of their salary (6.2% goes to Social Security, 1.45% goes to Medicare); employers pay 7.65%; self-employed pay 15.3%.

Medicare: This Social Security program, started in 1965, provides basic health insurance protection for people over age 65 and the permanently disabled. The plan covers hospitalization, doctor bills, testing, and prescriptions. Only the hospitalization insurance is free.

The best-known Social Security benefit is for retirement, which accounts for two-thirds of the agency's payouts. To qualify, a person must work 40 three-month periods in his or her career during which they earn at least a threshold (in 1994, $590). The benefits are based on the amount of money a person made in his or her career. Monthly benefits go no higher than $1,200 in 1995. Those approaching retirement have a choice at what age they can begin collecting Social Security retirement benefits in return for reduced or expanded benefits. Those born before 1937 get full benefits if they retire at age 65; 80% of benefits if they start collecting at age 62; and 120% of benefits if they wait until 70. New rules made in 1983 that helped financially stabilize the Social Security system pushed back the age when full benefits can be collected. For example, the new sliding scale makes 66 the full-benefit age for those born in 1945 through 1954 and 67, for those born after 1960. To see if your work has been properly credited, call Social Security at (800) 772-1213 and ask for Form 7004. When the is form filled out and returned to the agency, you'll get back a summary of your work history and an estimate of your retirement benefits. Or you can use the following chart as a rough estimate based on a worker retiring in 1995 at age 65 after steady lifetime income:

Earnings	Individual Benefits	Worker and Spouse Benefits
$20,000	$9,500	$14,100
$30,000	$12,500	$18,700
$40,000	$13,400	$20,100
$50,000	$14,000	$21,100
$57,600 or more	$14,200	$21,300

These figures represent annual amounts of income and benefits.

Disability: More than 4 million Americans under age 65 get Social Security benefits since they can no longer earn a living because they have physical ailments or are family members of the disabled. You must be unable to perform any work and be sick or injured for a year to collect.

Survivors' Benefits: Social Security acts like a life insurance plan, too. If you die young, your widow or widower and your children can get monthly checks until the children leave home. These benefits also cover widows and widowers of deceased retirees who were receiving benefits.

Auxiliary Benefits: Spouses or former spouses of retirees, who themselves are retired, can collect additional Social Security benefits in some cases. There are complex rules about who qualifies for these benefits.

Seeds for a Comfortable Retirement

This long-term planning guide can help you plan your retirement savings. You will be well served to use photocopies, since you may find yourself changing estimates and working out various scenarios. (Consult Chapter 23, "Compound Interest," and the "electronics notes" in this worksheet for help with using a financial calculator or computer spreadsheet program with this worksheet.) This guide can also be used for other long-term savings goals, such as educational expenses.

Step 1: Current Nest Egg

Add up the value of all retirement savings. Include IRAs (individual retirement accounts); employer-sponsored plans such as 401(k), 403(b), and 457 plans, or any other money you have targeted for your retirement.

> 1

Step 2: Your Pensions

Will your household be getting any traditional pension benefits from any employers? Ask your employers' benefits department for an estimate of expected benefits. For younger workers, this may be of little help. You could estimate that many typical pensions pay benefits equal to 1% of average annual pay for each year employed. Annualize any benefits (multiply monthly benefits by 12, for example), and try to keep the estimate in current or today's dollars.

> 2

Step 3: Social Security

Call the Social Security Administration at (800) 772-1213 and ask for Benefits Estimate Form 7004. Fill it out and return it to the agency, which will send back to you an estimate of your retirement benefits. You can also look at the chart in the previous illustration to make a quick estimate. Annualize any benefits and try to keep the estimate in current dollars.

> 3

Step 4: Income You'll Need

Now you must estimate your living expenses in retirement. There are two ways to do this.

The easy way is to guess that you will need between 60% and 100% of your household's current after-tax income during retirement. Variables in this estimate include housing costs (Do you own a home clear of debt?) or medical costs (Are you healthy? Well-insured?). Such estimates are best for younger people.

The hard way is to do a thorough review of all expected expenses during retirement. (The cash-flow worksheet in Chapter 24, "Planning Your Financial Road Map," can help.) Remember to include expenses such as taxes and medical insurance. A detailed approach is best for people close to retirement.

In either case, annualize any benefits and try to keep the estimate in current dollars.

> 4

Step 5: Investment Returns

Now you have to estimate how much you expect your retirement nest egg investments to earn. You will need this number to tabulate how money accumulates while you are saving for retirement, and how your money is dispensed once you've stopped working. (You can use a different number for the accumulation and distribution periods.)

To help you pick a reasonable goal, here's a look at average profits for three portfolios of stocks from 1943 to 1994.

Portfolios	50-Year Average	Best Year	Worst Year
Lower risk (15% stocks, 20% bonds, 65% cash)	6.1%	18.6%	–0.5%
Moderate risk (55% stocks, 20% bonds, 25% cash)	9.3%	28.8%	–13.8%
Higher risk (85% stocks, 15% bonds, 0% cash)	11.4%	44.6%	–23.2%

Note that during this period, stocks (measured by Standard & Poor's 500) averaged 12.3% annual profits, bonds (measured by corporate bond index) averaged 5.6% annual profits, and cash (measured by Treasury bills) averaged 4.6%.

> 5a

But there's a catch! Inflation plays an enormous role in retirement planning. To be conservative, you have to translate your profit estimates to reflect how inflation cuts into your buying power. You must estimate what inflation will be (it averaged 4.3% a year from 1943 to 1994) and subtract that figure from your estimated profits to get an after-inflation profit.

So, what's your inflation estimate?

> 5b

Subtract that estimate from projected profits (line 5a) to get projected after-inflation profits.

> 5c

Step 6: Retirement Calendar

When will you retire? How many years until you quit the daily grind? You will find that the longer you work, the less you'll need to save for retirement.

> 6a

Now you must estimate how long a retirement you will have to fund. It's a tough question. The Internal Revenue Service estimates that one member of a couple, both 65, will live for 25 years.

> 6b

Step 7: The Nest Egg You'll Need

Add up what income you plan to have during retirement. First, note your estimated annual retirement costs (line 4)

Subtract pension benefits (line 2)

Subtract Social Security benefits (line 3)

That equals your retirement income shortfall
7a

Taxes also play a big role in retirement planning. We have to figure out how much income you'll need to both pay taxes and live comfortably. First, jot down your income tax rate. (For middle-income people in states with income taxes it's around 33%.)
7b

Now divide the shortfall (line 7a) by the results of 1 minus the tax rate (line 7b) to get the pretax shortfall.
7c

Find your "distribution" factor from Chart A below. It will help you figure out how big a nest egg you need to pay for your retirement. The factor is found by matching your after-inflation expected profits (line 5c) and your estimated retirement length (line 6b).
7d

Chart A: After-Inflation Returns

Years	2%	4%	6%	8%
5	4.713	4.452	4.212	3.993
10	8.983	8.111	7.36	6.71
15	12.849	11.118	9.712	8.559
20	16.351	13.59	11.47	9.818
25	19.523	15.622	12.783	10.675
30	22.396	17.292	13.765	11.258
35	24.999	18.665	14.498	11.655

(Electronics note: This is a present value calculation where "years" is retirement length, "payment" is the shortfall, "percent" is after-inflation profits, and "future value" is 0.)
Now multiply that shortfall (line 7c) by the distribution factor (line 7d) to get the required nest egg.
7e

Step 8: Growing Your Current Nest Egg

Your retirement savings to date will play a role in your planning. First, jot down your nest egg total (line 1)
8a

Next, find your "growth" factor in Chart B. Match your estimated after-inflation profits (line 5c) and your years until retirement (line 6b) to get the factor.

Chart B: After-Inflation Profits

Years	2%	4%	6%	8%
1	1.02	1.04	1.06	1.08
2	1.04	1.082	1.124	1.166
3	1.061	1.125	1.191	1.26
4	1.082	1.17	1.262	1.36
5	1.104	1.217	1.338	1.469
10	1.219	1.48	1.791	2.159
15	1.346	1.801	2.397	3.172
20	1.486	2.191	3.21	4.661
25	1.641	2.666	4.292	6.848
30	1.811	3.243	5.743	10.063
35	2	3.946	7.686	14.785

(Electronics note: This is a "future value" calculation where "years" is years to retirement, "present value" is current nest egg, "percent" is after-inflation profits, and "payment" is 0.)
Now multiply the current nest egg by the Chart B growth factor (line 8a) to get what your current nest egg will be worth at retirement in current dollars.
8b

Step 9: How Much You Are Short

First jot down the required nest egg (line 7e)

Subtract the new value of the current nest egg (line 8b)

To get the nest egg shortfall
9

Step 10: How Much to Save

The last chore is getting a "payment" factor from Chart C. Match your estimated after-inflation profits (line 5c) and your years to retire (line 6a).
10

Chart C: After-Inflation Profits

Years	2%	4%	6%	8%
1	0.98	0.962	0.943	0.926
2	0.485	0.471	0.458	0.445
3	0.32	0.308	0.296	0.285
4	0.238	0.226	0.216	0.206
5	0.188	0.178	0.167	0.158
10	0.09	0.08	0.072	0.064
15	0.057	0.048	0.041	0.034
20	0.04	0.032	0.026	0.02
25	0.031	0.023	0.02	0.013
30	0.024	0.017	0.012	0.008
35	0.02	0.013	0.009	0.005

(Electronics note: This is a "payment" calculation where "years" is years to retirement, "future value" is nest egg short fall, "percent" is after-inflation profits, and "present value" is 0.)
Multiply the payment factor (line 10) by the nest egg shortfall (line 9) to find out how much you must save a year to meet your retirement goals.

REVAMPING
YOUR FINANCES

CONTENTS

Chapter 23: Compound Interest: The Most Powerful
Element of Finance
150

Chapter 24: Planning Your Financial Road Map
154

Chapter 25: Why $1 Million Isn't What It Used to Be
166

LIKE MANY HOUSEHOLD chores, managing one's money can't be put off forever. Sooner or later, however, a poorly thought out financial plan will cost you. And even if you've been doing it for a while, there are so many new products and twists to the financial world that a refresher course may be in order.

Don't put off a financial makeover because it sounds like a lot of work that needs to be constantly updated. While it is important to get a good snapshot of your finances at regular intervals, once a year would suffice. You don't need to feel inadequate if you can't keep up with a neighbor who diligently keeps track of every household expense and adjusts his or her investment portfolio monthly.

You'll need a good collection of your financial records to start. How you file all that paperwork isn't very important, but a new file cabinet wouldn't be a bad investment. You'll also need some way to track your finances. Paper and pencil will do fine, but electronics will help greatly. A plain calculator will ensure that your math is correct. A business calculator with financial functions will give you great flexibility in plotting your financial plan and when making major purchases with credit.

A computer is not a necessity just to do home finances. If you already own a computer, any basic financial spreadsheet program will do the trick of tabulating and dissecting your finances. There are also several well-designed home-finance specialty programs like Intuit's Quicken or Meca's Managing Your Money that cater to a home-grown financial plan. If you're relatively computer proficient, you'll find that you can use a modem telephone hookup to pay bills or track your investments.

Once you understand your financial picture, you'll want to know what to do next. That can often entail learning more about money than this or any one publication can provide. Educating yourself about money is a constant process in today's ever-changing financial system. You could give this responsibility to trusted advisers, but if they are any good, they will insist upon your participation in the decision-making process anyway.

One good way to start getting smart about money is by reading periodicals. Newspapers, magazines, and newsletters provide news on investments and money matters, and serve as a good source of background material. Take what's written by the financial press with skepticism, though. (I should know, I've been a business journalist since 1983.) Journalists are just as vulnerable to getting caught up with a herd mentality about money trends as are professional traders or even novice investors. In fact, some experts believe the financial press can be used as a contrarian indicator, that is, to buy when news reports say "sell" and vice versa. So learn to separate news of short-term fluctuations in investment markets from sound and sensible money management advice. Don't jump to the conclusion that money advice in print must be right for you.

National newspapers as well as many local papers are devoting a greater amount of their business coverage to personal finance issues. One trick is to find out what day of the week those stories are printed. The nation's major financial daily newspaper, the *Wall Street Journal*, is an especially good source of money management ideas on Fridays, when the paper focuses on basic financial issues. Many local papers beef up their personal finance coverage on Sundays or Mondays.

There are a slew of financial magazines that provide good coverage of pocketbook issues. The best known is *Money* magazine, which practically invented money-management journalism. Today, *Money* has stiff competition from magazines such as *Kiplinger's Personal Finance, Smart Money,* and *Worth. Barron's,* a sister weekly publication to the *Wall Street Journal,* has a wealth of facts and figures, but it is best suited for experienced investors. Traditional business magazines like *Forbes* and *Business Week* offer personal finance news, as does *Consumer Reports* and *U.S. News & World Report.* With magazines, be wary of cover stories boasting of ways to make you rich.

Investment newsletters typically cater to a small audience of sophisticated investors. Each newsletter editor has a unique system that picks what he or she believes are the best investments available. Subscriptions can be pricey, $200 or more a year, and there's often little of educational value in these publications. Unless you are just looking for the right place to put your money, most newsletters should be considered a luxury.

If you want a more detailed view of money, there are many books that can boost your financial IQ. So take a trip to the library or bookstore and check out titles such as *Making the Most of Your Money* by well-known columnist Jane Bryant Quinn (published by Simon & Schuster); *Funding Your Future: The Only Guide to Mutual Funds You'll Ever Need* by *Wall Street Journal* reporter Jonathan Clements (Warner Books); *Barron's Guide to Making Investment Decisions* by two *Wall Street Journal* reporters, Douglas Sease and John Prestbo (Prentice Hall); and *One Up on Wall Street* by famous investor Peter Lynch (Penguin Books).

One last source of information about money matters is the financial industry itself. Many reputable financial-service companies offer excellent educational guides. Topics include everything from getting a home loan to dealing with credit card problems to buying stocks or mutual funds. Best of all, they are usually free. So if there's a money product you are interested in, call the company and ask if they have any educational materials on the subject.

Compound Interest: The Most Powerful Element of Finance

COMPOUND INTEREST (or "compounding") builds great wealth by repeatedly piling current interest gains on top of previous gains. It is also the culprit that creates huge debts when interest costs are similarly amassed.

In wealth-building situations, compounding makes interest or percentage gains on an investment worth more as interest is paid both on the original investment and on previous interest or gains. For example, if 6 percent annual interest is compounded monthly (that is, 6 percent paid in 12 equal parts, or half a percent a month), it's actually worth 6.17 percent for the year. So, $10,000 would grow to $10,617 under this compounding method. If "straight" or "simple" interest (paid only once and only on the investment) had been used, $10,000 would grow to just $10,600.

Compounding's biggest wealth-building power comes over lengthy periods. It magnifies slight differences in interest rates to large advantages. For example, say one investor earns 6 percent, compounded monthly, on $25,000 for 20 years. A second investor with the same investment goals earns 7 percent. At the end, the first investor has $82,755, while the second has $100,968. Compounding made the second investor's "straight" interest advantage of $5,000 (1 percent a year on $25,000, or $250, for 20 years) worth $18,213.

When it comes to paying interest on loans, compounding can be painful. It leads many people to feel that they can't get out from under their debts as interest charged on interest balloons the amount owed to the bank. Compounding is why it is so important to minimize high-rate debts like those from credit cards and finance companies. For example, a $2,000 purchase made with expensive credit will double in cost within four years at 17 percent a year interest (the 1994 average for major credit cards). Even if you pay $100 a month toward this purchase, it will take two years, or $2,400, to pay it off completely at 17 percent.

There's one trick, the "Rule of 72," that can help you understand compounding's power. Take an interest rate, divide it into 72, and you'll find out roughly how many years it takes for money to double. It works for either investments or debts. So, at 6 percent (6 divided into 72), money doubles roughly every 12 years. At 12 percent, money doubles every six years.

How to Make Financial Calculations

Learn how to use a financial calculator, or the financial functions of a personal computer spreadsheet program. Not only will it give you great insight into compound interest, but it also will allow you to better plan your finances or bargain for investments or loans. Here is a look at the five key elements of the basic compound interest equation, as they might appear on a financial calculator and in Microsoft's Excel and Lotus's 1-2-3 spreadsheet programs. Typically, you'll know four of the calculations and will only need to compute the fifth.

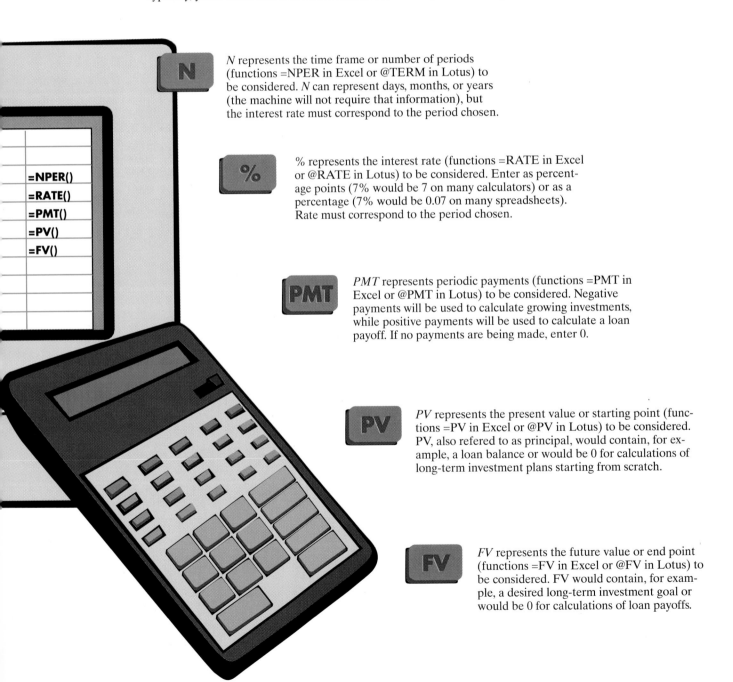

=NPER()
=RATE()
=PMT()
=PV()
=FV()

N — *N* represents the time frame or number of periods (functions =NPER in Excel or @TERM in Lotus) to be considered. *N* can represent days, months, or years (the machine will not require that information), but the interest rate must correspond to the period chosen.

% — % represents the interest rate (functions =RATE in Excel or @RATE in Lotus) to be considered. Enter as percentage points (7% would be 7 on many calculators) or as a percentage (7% would be 0.07 on many spreadsheets). Rate must correspond to the period chosen.

PMT — *PMT* represents periodic payments (functions =PMT in Excel or @PMT in Lotus) to be considered. Negative payments will be used to calculate growing investments, while positive payments will be used to calculate a loan payoff. If no payments are being made, enter 0.

PV — *PV* represents the present value or starting point (functions =PV in Excel or @PV in Lotus) to be considered. PV, also refered to as principal, would contain, for example, a loan balance or would be 0 for calculations of long-term investment plans starting from scratch.

FV — *FV* represents the future value or end point (functions =FV in Excel or @FV in Lotus) to be considered. FV would contain, for example, a desired long-term investment goal or would be 0 for calculations of loan payoffs.

Here are a few examples of how these compounding calculations can be helpful. (These examples are for calculators. Computer programs may handle data slightly differently. Check the user's manual.)

At the car dealership, Frank calculates his monthly payment for a new car by entering the monthly periods (60 on a five-year loan), an interest rate of 0.666 (8% divided by 12 months), his loan amount (a present value of $15,000), and future value of 0. He calculates a payment of $304.09. (Enter N=60; %=.666; PV=15,000; FV=0. Calculate PMT=304.09) To find out how much smaller payments would be with a bigger down payment, just change the present value (loan balance) and recalculate.

Doug and Marlene want to know much they need to earn on investments to retire in 15 years. They have $50,000 but feel they need $250,000 to retire comfortably. They can save $300 a month. Present value is $50,000, future value is $250,000, periods are 180 (15 times 12 months), and payment is –300. They calculate a rate of 0.61 a month or 7.4% a year. (Enter PV=50,000; FV=250,000; PMT=–300; N=180. Calculate %=.61.)

David and Judy need to save for their child's college education. They can save $200 a month. How much will they have in ten years? They enter payment as –200, present value as 0 (they're just starting out), periods as 120 (months), and they estimate they'll earn 9%—so the rate is 0.75 (9 divided by 12 to match monthly calculations). They calculate a future value of $38,702. (Enter PMT=–200; N=120; %=.75; PV=0. Calculate FV=36,591.)

Marianne is getting a credit card with a 12% rate to pay off a $3,000 balance on an 18% card. What will she save if she pays $100 a month? With her current card, present value is $3,000, payments are $100, future value is 0, and rate is 1.5 (18 divided by 12). The time calculated is 40 (months). For a new card, the rate becomes 1 (12 divided by 12). Recalculated time is 36 months. Four months at $100 is a $400 savings. (Enter PV=3,000; PMT=100; FV=0; %=1.5. Calculate N=40. Change %=1. Calculate N=36.)

CHAPTER 24

Planning Your Financial Road Map

GETTING A HANDLE on your personal finances means doing some homework. And there's no easy way or short cut to get your money plans going in the right direction.

To put your money on the right path, you first have to take a thorough inventory of your current financial picture. Collect recent statements from your employer, bankers, lenders, and investment managers, plus credit card, utility, and other major billings. You need to add up all your assets (things you own, from savings to stock to cars) and all your debts (bills and other regular obligations). You'll have to figure out where all your money is coming from, and more importantly and more difficult, where it's going.

Next, you have to figure out your financial goals. This is an extremely important exercise. Could you imagine taking a long trip without plans of how to travel, where you'll stay, and what you might do when you get to your destination? And with planning financial goals, you have the difficult chore of planning perhaps 30 years or more of saving, spending, and investing. But starting early always helps. Consider this scenario. Two families are working to save $50,000 for a child's education. One starts at the child's birth; the other when the child's 8. If both families earn 7 percent a year, the early starters have to sock away $116 a month. The family that starts later must save $289 a month.

Once you've gotten your financial picture and your goals arranged, you can review your savings and investing habits. You can check to see if you are putting away enough money and if it is going into the proper investments. Many people never get around to this type of self-examination. However, attaining many financial goals that seem unreachable just requires an early head start and a good sense of financial discipline.

If this seems like a lot of work, you are right. But in most cases, it pays off handsomely. Let's imagine that all this work allows you to add $50 a month to your retirement fund and invest it in such a way that you earn another 1 percent a year. At first glance, that might not seem to be a very profitable change. But for a person previously investing $250 a month and earning 7 percent a year, the new strategy over 20 years earns an extra $46,000.

Adding Up Your Financial Picture

No financial plan can succeed unless you know your current financial status. You'll need to collect several months of recent statements and billings from banks, employers, and investments. Then try your best to fill out these cash flow and net worth worksheets. Consider photocopying these pages so you can use the worksheets repeatedly.

Your Net Worth

Let's look at what an accountant would call your "balance sheet," a tabulation of all your assets and your debts. First add up what you own. To be safe, use conservative values, including subtracting any sales commissions of fees you would have to pay. Then add up any loans or payments you must pay to keep a possession, such as remaining car-lease costs if you've listed the car as an asset.

ASSETS	AMOUNT
Homes, Real Estate	$
Cars	
Savings accounts	
Investments	
Retirement plans	
Cash value insurance	
Other	

DEBTS	AMOUNT
Mortgages	$
Car loans	
Education loans	
Credit cards	
Personal loans	
Taxes due	
Other	

TOTAL ASSETS $

TOTAL DEBTS $

MINUS DEBTS − $

YOUR NET WORTH = $

Your Cash Flow

Let's check how you are doing keeping up with your cash flow. First, enter all your sources of income, from work to investments. You can do this as a monthly or annual figure, but make sure you use the same timeframe throughout this chart. Second, add up all your expenses, including taxes and savings. Then subtract income from expenses. A positive number means you have room to maneuver. A negative number can be a sign of trouble.

OUTFLOW/EXPENSES	AMOUNT
HOME	$
Mortgage	
Property taxes	
Rent	
Insurance	
Other	
BASICS	$
Food, dining out	
Clothing	
Cleaning	
Expected major purchase	
Entertainment	
Utilities	
Other	
TRANSPORTATION	$
Car payments	
Fuel	
Insurance	
Maintenance	
Transit fares	
Other	

OUTFLOW/EXPENSES cont.	AMOUNT
MISCELLANEOUS	$
Life, medical insurance	
Savings contributions	
Income taxes	
Other taxes	
Other major expenses	
Other	

TOTAL OUTFLOW $

INFLOW/INCOME	AMOUNT
Your salary	$
Other salary	
Other pay	
Pension/benefits pay	
Savings income	
Investment income	
Other income	
	$

TOTAL INCOME $

MINUS OUTFLOW − $

HOW YOU'RE DOING = $

How to Set Financial Goals

Once you have figured out how much you've got, the next chore is to figure out where you are going. Setting financial goals brings discipline to your financial planning. You will find that your financial goals will change throughout your life. Let's examine typical goals at various points in your life.

Young Singles: People in their 20s and early 30s have financial goals such as saving for a car, paying off student loans, building savings for a down payment on a first home, and slowly starting a retirement fund.

Young Families: With marriage and babies, financial goals change to emphasize saving for a down payment on a home, building a retirement fund, and starting savings for the children's college education.

Prime Timers: People in their 40s and 50s with teenage children face two huge financial goals: completing college financing and accelerating retirement savings. College usually gets most of the money.

Empty Nesters: Once the children have left home, and you're in your 50s or early 60s, most savings are plowed toward building the retirement fund and using strategies to lower tax bills. Other financial goals may be vacations or a second home.

Here's a look at some goals and how you can plan for them. Jot down the amount you want to save for each goal and the time you think it will take you to reach that goal. Check with the accompanying chart to figure out how much you must save each month to reach your goal.

Transportation

Goal: $
Years to goal:
Savings needed: $

+

Housing

Goal: $
Years to goal:
Savings needed: $

+

One way to manage your money is on a goal-by-goal basis. Choose a goal, figure the time you'll need to save that money, and then make the appropriate investments.

Less Than 2 Years
Best suited are mostly cash investments (bank accounts, Treasury bills, money funds, and short-term bond funds). Expected returns: 2–3% after tax.

2–5 Years
Best suited are a mix of cash, bonds (short-term and intermediate term), and some conservative stocks. Expected returns: 4–5% after tax.

5–10 Years
Best suited are a mix of bonds (short-term and intermediate term) and risk investments such as conservative and aggressive stocks and real estate. Expected returns: 5–7% after tax.

10 or More Years
Best suited are primarily conservative and aggressive stocks and real estate. Expected returns: 7–9% after tax.

This chart will show you what you'll need to save a month to reach $1,000 over various time frames at various rates of profits. To find a different size goal, just divide your goal by 1,000 and then multiply the result by the required savings from the chart. (Example: To reach $25,000, multiply the required savings by 25.) Also, remember that you'll have to pay taxes, so use after-tax returns—a middle-income family, for an estimate, can reduce expected profits by one-third to get after-tax returns.

Years to goal

Required monthly savings to goal / Annual profit	2	3	4	5	6	8	10	15	20	30
2%	$40.87	$26.98	$20.03	$15.86	$13.08	$9.61	$7.53	$4.77	$3.39	$2.03
4%	40.09	26.19	19.25	15.08	12.31	8.86	6.79	4.06	2.73	1.44
6%	39.32	25.42	18.49	14.33	11.57	8.14	6.10	3.44	2.16	1.00
8%	38.56	24.67	17.75	13.61	10.87	7.47	5.47	2.89	1.70	0.67
10%	37.81	23.93	17.03	12.91	10.19	6.84	4.88	2.41	1.32	0.44

Goals are nice. But can you reach them? Check to see if you can afford such savings, and if you can't, try to alter the timing of the events to make it work.

Education

Goal: $
Years to goal:
Savings needed: $

+

Retirement

Goal: $
Years to goal:
Savings needed: $

+

Other

Goal: $
Years to goal:
Savings needed: $

How Diversification Works

Every investor wants to find the one perfect investment to make the big profits. That's an almost impossible goal. First, finding such an investment is a crapshoot. Second, what if that investment turns out to be a bust? The most common advice to avoid the boom-or-bust dilemma is to diversify, often phrased as "not putting all your eggs in one basket." By spreading out among numerous investments, you reduce the chance that you'll get wiped out by a bad decision. Of course, diversification means a lesser chance of hitting it big.

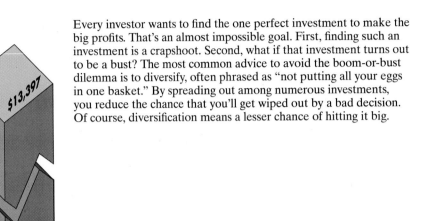

Here's a look at three scenarios for stock investors in 1992–1994: what if you invested $1,000 in what became one of the 15 most profitable U.S. stocks each of those three years (a roughly 1-in-700 shot); or in one of the worst 30 stocks; or in the 500 stocks of the Standard & Poor's 500 stock index.

Average profit for 30 best stocks:	$13,397
Average profit for S&P 500:	$37
Average loss for 30 worst stocks:	–$801

While the stock market has historically out-performed investments such as bonds and Treasury bills, there's no guarantee. So you have to spread your money around asset types, too. Look at this analysis of stocks, bonds, and T-bills from 1871 to 1994 and what was the best investment, looking at 1-month periods and 10-year periods (courtesy of American Strategic Capital of Los Alamitos, California).

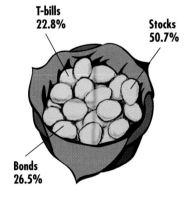

T-bills
22.8%

Stocks
50.7%

Bonds
26.5%

**Most Profitable in
1-Month Periods**

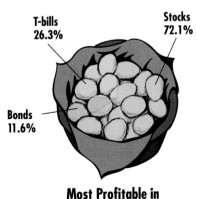

T-bills
26.3%

Stocks
72.1%

Bonds
11.6%

**Most Profitable in
10-Year Periods**

Another reason to diversify is to smooth out the bumpy roller-coaster ride investors can suffer through. The idea is to have some investments going up while a few are going down, giving your portfolio a more predictable path. Look at how $1,000 invested in stocks, homes, bonds, and cash has performed since 1987 and how an equal mix of each investment has done.

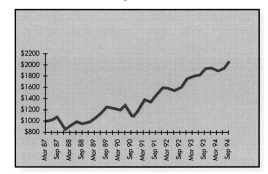

Stocks: Measured by the Standard & Poor's 500 index, zigged and zagged to profits that turned $1,000 into $2,054 in the period.

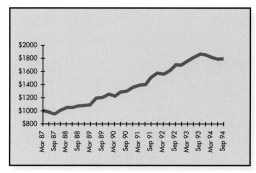

Bonds: Measured by an index of long-term bonds, went up then down, but left profits that turned $1,000 into $1,809 in the period.

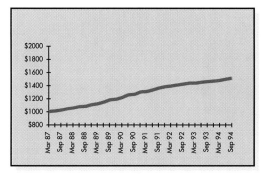

Cash: Measured by Treasury bill yields, made predictable profits that turned $1,000 into $1,514 in the period.

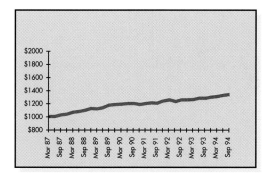

Real Estate: Measured by a national home price index from the Federal National Mortgage Association, rose slowly to profits that turned $1,000 into $1,342 in the period.

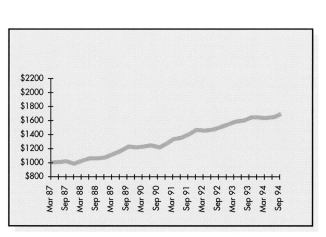

Diversified Mix: A portfolio of equal weightings of stocks, bonds, real estate, and cash had a smooth ride to profits that turned $1,000 into $1,580 in the period.

Asset Allocation: Recipe for Success

Asset allocation, the measure of the mix of investments in a portfolio, is considered one of the most important financial decisions you'll make. The calculation, used for both professionally managed and individuals' portfolios, typically comprises a mix of stocks, bonds, and cash. Other assets can be used, too. For example, real estate or metal investments can be lumped in with stocks. To find your asset allocation, add holdings of stocks, bonds and cash, and divide each sum by the total value of the portfolio. Figuring out how to allocate some of your investments for the calculation can be difficult. For example, with mutual funds that own both stocks and bonds, you'll have to find out what levels of stocks and bonds the fund holds. You can use the following grid, or a computer spreadsheet styled in such a fashion, to tabulate your asset allocation.

INVESTMENT	(A) Amount Dollars	(B) Percent Stock	(C) Percent Bonds	(D) Percent Cash	Dollars in Stock (A TIMES B)	Dollars in Bonds (A TIMES C)	Dollars in Cash (A TIMES D)
	$	%	%	%	$	$	$
	$	%	%	%	$	$	$
	$	%	%	%	$	$	$
	$	%	%	%	$	$	$
	$	%	%	%	$	$	$
	$	%	%	%	$	$	$
	$	%	%	%	$	$	$
	$	%	%	%	$	$	$
TOTAL the columns	(E) $				(F) $	(G) $	(H) $
Your Asset Allocation					STOCK PERCENT (F DIVIDED BY E) %	BOND PERCENT (G DIVIDED BY E) %	CASH PERCENT (H DIVIDED BY E) %

So what is the right asset allocation? It all depends on your sense of investment adventure and the amount of time you can hold these investments. Look at the following grid to find out what allocation might be best for you. (Investments to be held for less than two years should be totally in cash.)

RISK TOLERANCE VS. TIME HORIZON	2 to 5 years	5 to 10 years	More than 10 years
SKITTISH: Fearful of losses			
INCOME ORIENTED: Willing to take modest risks to earn good stream of income.			
GROWTH ORIENTED: Willing to take risks to grow investments			
AGGRESSIVE: Willing to take large risks.			

Now match your colored portfolio with the explanations below. The historical performance figures represent average profits for all 12-month periods from 1871 to September 1994 and were compiled by American Strategic Capital of Los Alamitos, California.

Blue—Very Conservative
A very conservative mix would emphasize safety and offer a steady stream of dividend payments. This portfolio would be heavy with bonds and hold lots of cash. There would be a little bit of stock to help investors stay ahead of inflation. But there's a price to pay for safety. Historical average return for a mix of 50% bonds, 30% cash, and 20% stocks is only 5.4% a year.

Green—Modestly Conservative
A modestly conservative mix would take some risks to get both capital gains and a stream of dividend payments. This portfolio would bet equally on bonds and stocks, with some cash holdings. It's a fair trade for the risk-averse investor. Historical average return for a mix of 40% bonds, 40% stocks, and 20% cash is 6.9% a year.

Red—Modestly Aggressive
A modestly aggressive mix would emphasize growth of investments while producing a small stream of income. This portfolio would be strong weighted toward stocks with some bonds and a small amount of cash. Such portfolios have been good performers. Historical average return for a mix of 60% stocks, 30% bonds, and 10% cash is 7.1% a year.

Black—Aggressive
An aggressive mix would seek the highest potential growth on the money invested, a strategy best suited for investors who tolerate risk or have extended investment horizons. This portfolio bets heavily on stocks while holding some bonds and little or no cash. The rewards can be great. Historical average return for a mix of 80% stocks and 20% bonds is 8.8% a year.

Frauds: How Not to Be a Victim

You work hard for your money, why fall victim to a con artist? Fraudulent businesses take billions from consumers every year in schemes that see Americans lose money in everything from investments in nonexistent gold mines or worthless rights to high technology products to paying steep fees for phony contests or loans. The following is a checklist of items you should consider before turning over your money to someone, and a review of some common scams.

Do Remember: No Free Lunch
If it's too good to be true, it probably is. No risk. Big payoff. Virtually guaranteed. You may wish it were true, but check very carefully. Con artists can't hoodwink you with an "average" sounding deal. If your gut says a deal sounds too good, better think about passing.

Don't Be Rushed into a Deal
Don't let a con artist pressure you into a decision. The hard-sell approach can force you to "act before this offer ends" or sells out. If you're not comfortable with a deal, don't let a deadline force you into saying "Yes."

Do Keep Your Guard Up
Some con artists use a soft touch, especially when they target the elderly. These salespeople will be chatty, ask about the family, buy you coffee and pastries—then stick you. Don't let your guard down just because someone is "pleasant."

Don't Give Money to Strangers
Be wary of a sales pitch from an unknown entity on the telephone. And think twice before dialing a "900" number that can cost you big bucks to win a prize. Don't give out credit card numbers or send money without carefully reviewing written details of an offer.

Do Understand the Risks
Check the promised return of supposedly "guaranteed" investments against those of Treasury bills or bank accounts. If the investment you're being pitched is earning substantially more than T-bills or CDs, that "guaranteed" offer includes much more risk.

Don't Fall for Once-in-a-Lifetime Deals
The chances of a stranger offering a legitimate rare investment opportunity that will pan out are slim. There are too many honest professional investment experts searching the globe for great deals for you to be so lucky to get offered a true chance to get rich.

Do Your Homework
There are no shortcuts. Know what you're investing in. Check out any business or broker who you're going to give money. Call state or federal regulators or your local Better Business Bureau to see if the company is licensed and if there have been any complaints or sanctions on file.

Don't Give Anyone All Your Money
Diversification can protect you from the pain of a fraud. By spreading your investments among several companies (even if you're using a trusted advisor or major investment companies), you can never lose everything as has happened to some scam victims.

Do Complain if You've Been Scammed
Doing nothing won't get your money back. And what's worse, your silence will let the con artists continue their thievery. If something's gone wrong, and the company isn't responsive, call regulators, the police, and the Better Business Bureau where the company is located.

Don't Get Scammed Twice
One of the most insidious new frauds is called "reloading," where con artists share victims' names and telephone numbers. The second fraud is contacting the defrauded people and promising to help recover the losses for a fee. Of course, no detective work is ever done.

Here is a look at some common scams that are pitched to numerous Americans every day.

Pyramid: This fraud's name represents the shape of the organization that's required for the scam to work. A handful of early investors, often both con artists and unsuspecting people, promote a moneymaking club or network concept. The problem is that the scheme only makes money when new investors are constantly recruited. The business changes to primarily selling memberships into the club or network, which often prove to have marginal value. The last investors are often stuck with little or no chance to profit.

Ponzi: This fraud is named after Charles Ponzi, who conned people in Boston in the 1920s with supposedly valuable stamps. The hook to a Ponzi scheme involves con artists promoting a supposedly lucrative investment idea and delivering attractive profits to early investors. Meanwhile, the scammers pay themselves fat salaries. The Ponzi collapses when the scam's backbone, the flow of new investors whose money is going to pay old investors rather than go into any investments, dries up.

Boiler Room: Named for the high-pressure sales tactics used by scamming telemarketers. These con artists use polished scripts to call thousands of targets and convince a handful to send money to get into a purportedly hot investment or buy valuable goods at supposedly discounted prices. But the story ends when the crooks pick up their business and move elsewhere, leaving the customer with worthless investments or overpriced merchandise.

Prize Scam: This scam is all about what you don't win and what it costs you. Con artists contact their targets, either by telephone or mail, and tell potential victims that they've won a fabulous prize. But there's a catch: a "winner" must pay a steep "processing" fee in advance, or call a high-cost "900" long-distance telephone number to get more details. Eventually, the "winner" turns "loser" when there's no prize, or one worth a fraction of the money given to the prize promoter.

CHAPTER
25

Why $1 Million Isn't What It Used to Be

ONE MILLION DOLLARS is a lot of money in today's world. In 1995 it would buy you ten average American houses or 50 typical new cars. It even would finance an extremely comfortable retirement. But many factors are quickly making the thought of collecting $1 million of savings more a goal than a dream for many Americans. Inflation (the rise in the cost of living) makes $1 million worth less each year. And over longer periods, inflation can dramatically reduce buying power. Goods that cost $1 million in 1965 cost five times that in 1995. In addition, the cloudy future of the nation's Social Security system and many corporate pension plans make saving a large sum a necessity for many people. Experts predict that money shortages will force government and business pension benefits to be reduced in coming years. Alternatives to these traditional sources of retirement income force the individual to make the tough investment decisions. So putting money away in IRAs (individual retirement accounts), employer-offered 401(k) plans, and life insurance companies' annuity programs means that many Americans must learn how to manage a six-figure, or even a seven-figure, portfolio of investments.

If you had $1 million sitting in your retirement nest egg and were ready to exit the work force today, you'd be in pretty good shape. If you financed a 20-year retirement with $1 million today, you could expect your nest egg to generate on average $66,707 of 1995 buying power. That assumes that you'd earn 7 percent a year on your investments and that inflation ran at 4 percent each year. On top of that there'd be government and/or employer retirement benefits.

The picture gets a little less rosy for younger folks looking at a million-dollar nest egg. If you were to reach $1 million in savings when you retired in 2005, using those same assumptions, you'll find that due to inflation, your buying power would be cut by roughly one-third. With a $1 million nest egg, a retiree in 2005 can expect 20 years of income averaging $45,065 in 1995 buying power.

People hoping to retire in 20 years would find that a $1 million nest egg generates only $30,444 in 1995 buying power using the same assumptions. And those 30 years away from retirement can only expect $20,567 in 1995 buying power from their million-dollar retirement nest egg. Imagine living on that income and getting reduced, or eliminated, pension benefits. Being a retired millionaire with $1 million in the bank may not buy you much caviar in 2025.

How to Make a Million

You might need $1 million more than you think. As inflation eats away at the buying power of $1 million, many investors will be forced to look at millionaire status as a requirement for a satisfying retirement. Getting to $1 million requires setting aside a large amount of money, letting investments grow for a long time, taking high risks to earn big profits on your investments, or a combination of the three. The following chart details how varying the amount of money invested monthly or the percentage of profits you earn on average each year alters how many years it will take to reach $1 million. To account for the tax bill you'll have to pay, assume your profit rate in after-tax percentages.

	Monthly Investments						
	$100	*$250*	*$500*	*$1,000*	*$2,000*	*$5,000*	*$10,000*
Average annual profits	Years to $1 Million						
4%	*90.2*	*67.9*	*51.9*	*37.4*	*25.0*	*13.0*	*7.3*
6%	*67.5*	*52.2*	*41.2*	*30.7*	*21.5*	*11.9*	*7.0*
8%	*54.8*	*43.1*	*34.6*	*26.5*	*19.1*	*11.0*	*6.6*
10%	*46.5*	*37.1*	*30.1*	*23.4*	*17.2*	*10.3*	*6.4*
12%	*40.7*	*32.8*	*26.9*	*21.2*	*15.8*	*9.7*	*6.1*
15%	*34.6*	*28.1*	*23.3*	*18.6*	*14.2*	*9.0*	*5.8*
20%	*28.1*	*23.1*	*19.4*	*15.8*	*12.3*	*8.0*	*5.4*
25%	*23.9*	*19.9*	*16.8*	*13.8*	*10.9*	*7.4*	*5.0*
30%	*21.1*	*17.6*	*15.0*	*12.4*	*9.9*	*6.8*	*4.8*
40%	*17.3*	*14.6*	*12.5*	*10.5*	*8.5*	*6.1*	*4.4*

How difficult is it to consistently earn 20% or more? The best 10-year period for the U.S. stock market, 1949–59, saw average profits of 21%. And the best stock mutual fund in the 10-year period of 1984–94, Twentieth Century Giftrust, averaged 22% profits. Basically, it's a pretty rare occurrence.

Time is an ally when trying to amass a fortune. The tortoise may not win the race, but it certainly has an easier time than those who try to sprint to a big investment goal. Here's a look at three time periods and recipes for how you might make your goal of $1 million.

$1 MILLION

10 Years

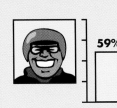

59%

This is a drag race. You either must start with lots of money, invest lots of money, take huge amounts of risk and be consistently correct, or be extremely lucky. The most likely strategy is to make a handful of big, winning bets. And how lucky must you be? If you started with $2,500 in 1984 and each New Year's Day for ten years moved your money into the mutual fund that was to become that year's most profitable investment, you had $1 million by 1994. But the chance of anyone choosing ten top funds in a row is about zero.

If you invest $500 a month, to get $1 million you must average annual profits of…59%

20 Years

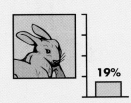

19%

You'll have to earn profits as quickly as a rabbit runs to make $1 million in 20 years. You must either generously invest or take sizable risks to generate large profits. To reach your goal, you'll likely need to place bets on risky investments such as stocks of newer, smaller U.S. companies, stocks from overseas companies, or real estate holdings. With two decades to work with, however, you'll be able to make many smaller bets—and you can afford some losses.

If you invest $500 a month, to get $1 million you must average annual profits of…19%

30 Years

10.1%

A tortoise-like approach can be used to make $1 million over 30 years. By investing a modest amount into moderately risky investments, you can reach this goal. For example, if you invest $500 a month, you only have to earn 10.1% a year to make $1 million in 30 years. That's roughly the average stock market profit since 1926. This is why financial planning experts urge people to start their long-term savings plans as early as possible.

If you invest $500 a month, to get $1 million you must average annual profits of…10.1%

A

adjustable-rate loans, 17–18, 124–125

agency bonds, 89

American Express card, 63

American Telephone and Telegraph (AT&T)

  credit card branch, 23

  effect of break-up, 3

Amex Computer Technology index, 115

Amex Institutional index, 114

Amex Major Market index, 114

Amex Oil index, 115

annuities, insurance, 130–131

asset allocation, 162–163

asset allocation fund, 106

ATMs (automated teller machines), 45, 55, 59

automobile insurance, 129–130, 132

B

bank accounts, 45–47

bank cards, 59. *See also* ATMs

  how they work, 60–61

banking regulations, establishment of, 9

Bank Network News newsletter, 59

bankruptcy, how it works, 38–39

banks

  regulatory agencies, 14

  types of, 13, 42–43

bank transactions, how they are recorded, 46–47

Barron's, 149

bear market, 82

Bloomberg Business News, compilation of interest-yield curve from, 52–53

blue chip funds, 104

boiler-room fraud schemes, 165

bond funds, 105

bond market

  playing, 76–77

  pros and cons, 89–91

  regulators, 9–11

bonds

  callability of, 93

  convertibility of, 93

  how to shop for, 92–93

  pros and cons of different types, 89–91

  subordination of, 93

book value, 81

brokers, stock, 12

bull market, 82

Business Week, 149

C

callability of bonds, 93

Canada's TSE 300 Composite index, 115

cash-flow worksheet, 157

cash investments, 95

casualty insurance, property, 12

certificates of deposit (CDs), 45, 95

CFTC (Commodity Futures and Trading Commission), 14

check clearinghouses, how they work, 56–57

checking accounts, 45

   evolution of, 55

closed-end funds, 12

commercial paper investments, 95

commodities market. *See also* commodity

   trading

   exchanges, 13

   how it works, 99

   regulators, 9–11, 14

Commodity Futures and Trading Commission

   (CFTC), 14

commodity trading, 100–101

competition, in economic marketplace, 2–3

compound interest, 151

   how to figure, 152–153

computer software, financial, 148

Consumer Price Index, tracking cost of living

   with, 36–37

Consumer Reports, 149

convertibility, of bonds, 93

corporate bonds, 89–90

credit bureaus, 71. *See also* credit reports

credit cards

   cost of providing to consumers, 50

   effects of deregulation on, 19–20

   how they changed the world, 63

   how they work, 64–65

credit reports

   contents of, 72–73

   how they work, 71

credit unions, 13, 14

currency, 5, 7

   faces on denominations, 6

cyclical stocks, 81

D

debenture, 92

defense spending, effect on economy, 34–35

demand, impact on economy, 2

depressions. *See* recessions and depressions

deregulation

   effect on credit cards, 19–20

   effect on financial deals, 17–20

   how it changed the money landscape, 22–23

disability insurance, 130

discount stock brokerages, 12

   effects of deregulation on, 19

diversification, how it works, 160–161

dividends, 80

dollar. *See* U.S. dollar

Dow Jones Industrial Average (the Dow),

   113, 114

Dow Jones Precious Metals index, 115

Dow Jones Transportation Average, 113, 115

Dow Jones World index, 115

E

early withdrawal penalties, 45

earnings per share, 80–81

economic booms and busts
causes of, 33-35
how bankruptcy works, 38–39
how inflation happens, 36–37
employment, effect on economy, 33–35
exchanges, 13. *See also specific names*

F

401(k) retirement plans, 22, 119, 136–137
advantages of, 140–141
403(b) plans, 137
advantages of, 140–141
457 programs, 137
advantages of, 140–141
faces, on U.S. currency, 6
FDIC (Federal Deposit Insurance Corp.),
9–11, 14
federal deposit insurance, 9–11
Federal Open Market Committee (FOMC)
composition of, 26
duties of, 27
Federal Reserve Banks, letter/number codes
on currency, 6
Federal Reserve Board (the Fed), 3, 14
formation of, 5, 55
Federal Reserve Notes, 5
Federal Reserve System (the Fed)
check-clearing system, 56–57
how it manages the economy, 26–27
power of, 25

Federal Trade Commission (FTC), 3, 10–11,
15
financial goals, setting, 158–159
financial planning, 148–149, 155
fiscal policies, 25
fixed annuity, 131
fixed-rate loans, 17, 124–125
Forbes magazine, 149
foreign bonds, 90
foreign currencies, 18
France's CAC-40 index, 115
frauds, 164–165
FTC (Federal Trade Commission), 10–11, 15
full-service stock brokerages, 12
funds, types of, 12

G

Germany's Dax index, 115
global investing, 86–87
global or world funds, 105
gold, 18
effect of deregulation on, 20
Gold Certificates, 5, 6
government, role of in economic marketplace,
2–3
Great Seal of the United States, 7
greenbacks. *See* United States Notes
gross domestic product (GDP), 33–34
growth funds, 104
growth stocks, 81

H

health (medical) insurance, 131, 133

health-maintenance organizations (HMOs), 131

high-yield funds (junk bonds), 106

home insurance, 130, 133

home loans, 17–18. *See also* mortgage rates

keys to getting, 124–125

tax deduction for interest paid, 23

home ownership, 121–123

housing, 13

regulatory agency for, 15

HUD (federal Department of Housing and Urban Development), 15

hybrid loans, keys to getting, 124–125

I

indexes. *See* stock market, indexes; *specific names*

inflation

causes of, 33–35, 36–37

controlling, 26–27

effect on interest rates, 49–51

insurance, 12, 129

annuities, 130–131

automobile, 129–130, 132

deductibles, 129

disability, 130

federal deposit, 9–11

health (medical), 12, 131, 133

home, 130, 133

life, 12, 130–131, 132

premiums, 129

property casualty, 12

rating agencies, 133

shopping for, 132–133

state regulatory agency, 15

types of, 129–131

insurers, 12, 13

interest expense, tax deduction for, 23

interest rates, 49–51

how they are figured, 52–53

intermediate-term interest rates, 53

inverted yield curve, 53

investment brokerages, regulation of, 10–11

investment business, 9

global, 86–87

publications about, 149

Investment Company Act of 1940, 103

investments, diversification of, 160–161

investment scams. *See* frauds

international funds, 105

IRAs (Individual Retirement Accounts), 23, 136–137

J

Japanese stock market, 113, 115

junk bonds, 106

K

Keoghs, 137

Kiplinger's Personal Finance, 149

L

legal tender, 5

life insurance, 12, 130–131, 132

Lipper Growth Fund index, 115

liquidity, 45

load funds, 103

loans. *See also* home loans; mortgage rates

   adjustable rate, 17–18

   fixed rate, 17

   how approval process works, 67–69

long-distance phone rates, effect of
      competition on, 3

long-term interest rates, 53

low-load funds, 103

luxury tax, effect on economy, 3

M

markets, playing, 76–77

MasterCard. *See* credit cards

medical (health) insurance, 12, 131, 133

Medicare program, 131, 142

monetary policy, 25, 26

money, 5–7

   how to make $1 million, 168–169

   the price of, 49–51

money funds. *See* money-market mutual
      funds

Money magazine, 149

money management, 118–119

   revamping your finances, 148–149

money-market mutual funds, 18, 45, 95,
      103–104

Morgan Stanley EAFE index, 115

mortgage

   bankers, 13

   bonds, 89

mortgage money, how it is made, 126–127

mortgage rates, 13, 17–18

   how they are figured, 50

municipal bonds, tax free, 29, 90

municipal funds, 105–106

mutual funds, 12, 79, 103–106

   choosing, 110–111

   how they work, 108–109

   money-market, 18, 95

   Net Asset Value (share price) of open-end
         funds, 108

   regulating agencies, 14

N

NAIC (National Association of Insurance
      Commissioners), 15

NASAA (North American Securities
      Administrators Association), 15

NASD (National Association of Securities Dealers), 13

Nasdaq (National Association of Securities Dealers Automated Quotations), 13, 84

Nasdaq Composite Index, 113, 114

National Bureau of Economic Research, 34

National Futures Association (NFA), 14

NCUA (National Credit Union Administration), 14

NCUSIF (National Credit Union Share Insurance Fund), 14

net worth balance sheet, 156

NFA (National Futures Association), 14

Nikkei 225 index, 113, 115

no-load funds, 103

note, 92

NYSE (New York Stock Exchange), 15

NYSE Financial index, 115

O

OCC (Office of the Comptroller of the Currency), 14

open-end funds, 12, 103

  Net Asset Value (share price) of, 108

OTS (Office of Thrift Supervision), 14

over-the-counter exchanges, 13

P

passbook accounts, 45

P/E (price-to-earnings) ratio, 80–81

Pension Benefit Guarantee Corp., 10, 136

pension plans, how they work, 138–139

PIN (personal identification number), 59

point-of-sale (POS) terminals, making purchases at, 59

Ponzi schemes, 165

preferred provider organizations (PPOs), 131

price-and-wage controls, 22

prices, impact on supply and demand for goods, 2

prize scams, 165

property-casualty insurance, 12

publications, financial, 149

pyramid schemes, 165

R

real estate
  agents, 13
  regulatory agency for, 15

recessions and depressions, causes of, 33–35

regulations (rule), for financial-services industry, 9–11

regulatory agencies, overview of, 14–15

retirement planning, 135–137, 144–145

retirement plans, 22, 23, 119
  401(k), 22, 119, 136–137
  403(b), 137
  457, 137

Russell 2000 index, 114

S

savings account, 45–47

savings banks, 13

savings and loans (S&Ls), 13

  effect of deregulation on, 18–19

  regulatory agencies, 14

scams. *See* frauds

seal, on currency, 7

SEC (U.S. Securities and Exchange Commission), 10–11, 14, 15

SEP-IRAs, 137

shares (stock), 79

shortest-term rates (interest), 53

short-term rates (interest), 53

Silver Certificates, 5, 6

Smart Money magazine, 149

social security, 135–136

  how it works, 142–143

software, financial, 148

Standard & Poor's 500 index (S&P 500), 104, 113

Standard & Poor's Midcap 400 index, 114

State attorney general (AG), as retailing regulatory agent, 15

statement accounts, 45

stock brokers, 12

stock exchanges, 13

  regulating agency, 14

stock market

  effects of deregulation on, 19

  exchanges, 13

  how it works, 79–82

  how trades work, 84–85

  indexes, 113–115

  playing, 76–77

  regulators, 9–11, 14, 15

stocks, types of, 81–82

stock yield, 80

subordination of bonds, 93

supply, impact on economy, 2

T

tax deductions, for interest expense, 23

taxes, 29

  effect on economy, 3, 34–35

  how they work, 30–31

Tax Foundation of Washington, D.C., 29, 30

tax incentives, effect on economy, 29

title insurers, 13

T-bills. *See* Treasury bills

Treasuries. *See* U.S. Treasury bonds

Treasury bills (T-bills), 95

  how auctions work, 96–97

Treasury Direct program, 96–97

U

U.K.'s FT-SE 100 (Footsie) index, 115

unemployment, effect on economy, 33–35

United States Notes (greenbacks), 5

U.S. agencies and industry watchdogs, 11

U.S. dollar, 5, 6–7

U.S. Secret Service, as counterfeiting watchdogs, 6

U.S. Securities and Exchange Commission (SEC), 10–11, 14, 15

U.S. Treasury bonds, 5, 51, 89

U.S. Treasury seal, significance of color on money, 7

usury laws, 10

V

Value Line Composite index, 114

value stocks, 81–82

variable annuity, 130

Visa. *See* credit cards

W

Wall Street Journal, 149

Wilshire 5000 index, 114

worksheets

asset allocation, 162–163

cash flow, 157

current financial status, 156

how much house you can afford, 125

retirement planning, 144–145

setting financial goals, 158–159

Worth magazine, 149

Y

yield curves, 52–53

yield, from stock, 80

Introducing the Expanded Line of Lavishly Illustrated
"How It Works" Books from Ziff-Davis Press.

How Weather Works
ROB DEMILLO
Illustrated by PAMELA DRURY WATTENMAKER

WEATHER WATCHERS
See what's behind: Wind shear and other flight hazards ✳ The global warming controversy ✳ Weather on other planets ✳ Foibles of forecasting ✳ *and more*

ISBN: 1-56276-228-1
Price: $19.95

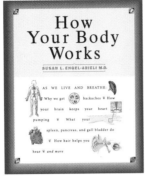

How Your Body Works
SUSAN L. ENGEL-ARIELI M.D.

AS WE LIVE AND BREATHE:
Why we get backaches ✳ How your brain keeps your heart pumping ✳ What your spleen, pancreas, and gall bladder do ✳ How hair helps you hear ✳ *and more*

ISBN: 1-56276-231-1
Price: $19.95

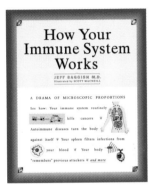

How Your Immune System Works
JEFF BAGGISH M.D.
Illustrated by SCOTT MACNEILL

A DRAMA OF MICROSCOPIC PROPORTIONS
See how: Your immune system routinely kills cancers ✳ Autoimmune diseases turn the body against itself ✳ Your spleen filters infections from your blood ✳ Your body "remembers" previous attackers ✳ *and more*

ISBN: 1-56276-233-8
Price: $19.95

How the Environment Works
PRESTON GRALLA
Illustrated by CHERIE PLUMLEE

SPOTLIGHT ON KEY ENVIRONMENTAL ISSUES:
The pros and cons of genetically engineering crops ✳ The explosion of the population bomb ✳ Design of nonpolluting landfills ✳ Anatomy of an oil spill ✳ *and more*

ISBN: 1-56276-232-X
Price: $19.95

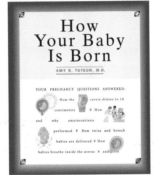

How Your Baby Is Born
AMY B. TUTEUR, M.D.

YOUR PREGNANCY QUESTIONS ANSWERED:
How the cervix dilates to 10 centimeters ✳ How and why amniocentesis performed ✳ How twins and breech babies are delivered ✳ How babies breathe inside the uterus ✳ *and more*

ISBN: 1-56276-239-7
Price: $19.95

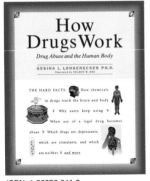

How Drugs Work
Drug Abuse and the Human Body
GESINA L. LONGENECKER PH.D.
Illustrated by NELSON W. HEE

THE HARD FACTS: How chemicals in drugs reach the brain and body ✳ Why users keep using ✳ When use of a legal drug becomes abuse ✳ Which drugs are depressants, which are stimulants, and which are neither ✳ *and more*

ISBN: 1-56276-241-9
Price: $19.95

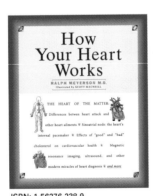

How Your Heart Works
RALPH MEYERSON M.D.
Illustrated by SCOTT MACNEILL

THE HEART OF THE MATTER: Differences between heart attack and other heart ailments ✳ Sinoatrial node: the heart's internal pacemaker ✳ Effects of "good" and "bad" cholesterol on cardiovascular health ✳ Magnetic resonance imaging, ultrasound, and other modern miracles of heart diagnosis ✳ *and more*

ISBN: 1-56276-238-9
Price: $19.95

This fall, Ziff-Davis Press raises health and science books to an art form with an exciting expansion of the "How It Works" concept that sold over 800,000 copies in its first 18 months.

Why do people love "How it Works"? It's easy to see. Self-contained layouts place an entire topic before the reader's eyes all at once on a set of facing pages. Dramatic, full-color graphics invite them to explore at their own pace. It's a concept so simple, so natural, you'd think it has been done before. It hasn't. Not like this.

How did we pull this off? We auditioned hundreds of authors to find the chosen few who know their stuff and can put it in writing. Backing them up are consulting editors who are equally expert in their field and gifted illustrators who combine topic knowledge with a passion for presentation.

Who reads "How It Works"? Everyone who ever felt too intimidated to ask a doctor a question. Everyone who ever marveled at the miracle of childbirth. Everyone who ever lost a picnic to an unforecast hailstorm. In fact, just about everyone.

Watch for many more subjects in the months ahead!
Available at all fine bookstores, or by calling 1-800-688-0448, ext. 261.

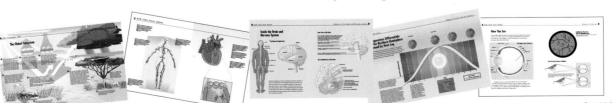

ZIFF-DAVIS
ZD
PRESS